SEASONAL
ITALIAN
favourites

Other related book titles available from *The Age* and *The Sydney Morning Herald* stores:
Seasonal by Steve Manfredi
Bistrode by Jane and Jeremy Strode
Guide to Fish by Hilary McNevin
Picnics edited by Karin Bishop
15 Minutes Flat by Lynne Mullins
Produce by Lynne Mullins
Baking edited by Kylie Walker
Seafood edited by Keith Austin
Blokes: Tasty No-fuss Recipes edited by Keith Austin
Eating Well by Tony Chiodo
Healthy Thai Cooking
Easy Japanese Cooking
The Age Cheap Eats
The Age Good Food Guide
The SMH Good Food Guide
The Foodies' Guide to Melbourne
The Foodies' Guide to Sydney
Plus a great range of lifestyle, travel, finance, sport and leisure books.

To find out more about these titles and other great offers please contact either:
The Age Shop on 1300 656 052 or www.theageshop.com.au
The SMH Shop on 1300 656 059 or www.smhshop.com.au

Copyright © 2009 Fairfax Media Publications Pty Ltd
1 Darling Island Road, Pyrmont NSW 2009

Publisher Fairfax Media Publications Pty Ltd
Designer and production manager Peter Schofield
Production editor Robyn Carter
Cover picture Jennifer Soo
Photography Jennifer Soo, Marco del Grande, Quentin Jones and Nicolas Walker

For distribution, copyright and marketing enquiries, contact Caroline Lowry on (02) 9282 3582

For production enquiries, contact Peter Schofield on (03) 9601 2149

Printed in China by i-Book Printing Ltd
ISBN 978-1-921486-07-4

SEASONAL
ITALIAN
favourites

STEFANO MANFREDI

Fairfax Books

SPRING

SUMMER

AUTUMN

WINTER

The whole world loves Italian food. But what is it that makes it so appealing? Well, firstly it travels the globe effortlessly. It seems to be at home in the tropics of Indonesia as much as it does in chilly England. It's unpretentious, easy to prepare and the recipes rely mostly on a relatively small number of ingredients. Sounds simple enough. But there's a catch.

If you've watched Italian chefs in a kitchen or, better still, one of their mothers or grandmothers, that seemingly effortless mastery is deceptive. Behind the scenes there is the inevitable army of growers, fishers, foragers and artisans that support *la vera cucina* (real Italian cooking). And, if it is a wonderful home-cooked meal, chances are the cook, the cook's family or friends will have grown some of the produce.

Above all, Italian cooking relies on the freshness of the produce, which is dictated by the seasons, and simple but skillful preparation. It doesn't rely on tricky presentation and complicated processes to distract from the prime ingredients.

This book adheres to the seasons because things taste better when they are at their peak. That is the primary reason but there are more. It's fundamentally logical to cook seasonally and doing so will save money and time.

Stefano Manfredi's restaurant
Bells at Killcare, New South
Wales.

Strawberries, for example, are available most of the year but in spring their perfume and flavour fill the fruit shops. This is their natural season. They are abundant and a fraction of the price at other times of the year. Spring is when strawberries should be made into jams and preserves.

You'll notice as you read through this book that I will mention outstanding varieties of particular produce such as rocket, zucchini, lemon and even sugar. This is yet another secret in the cook's arsenal. Using large spicy rocket leaves in a dish will give you far tastier results than with the ubiquitous "wild rocket".

A cursory flick through these pages will bring you across the occasional anomaly that seems to contradict the title. While it is a book primarily dealing with Italian dishes and how to cook them, there are a small number of recipes from other cuisines.

It's a small indulgence and a nod to living in Australia for so long. It's also recognition that Italian food is not a fixed notion but an evolving cuisine. Wherever it spreads, Italian cooking takes on some of the nuances of its adopted land but in essence it should remain true to its native principles.

Stefano Manfredi

Stefano Manfredi's restaurant Bells at Killcare, New South Wales.

SPRING

POTATOES

The United Nations declared 2008 International Year of the Potato. One of the key events in the calendar, the Global Potato Conference, was held in the historic city of Cuzco, Peru, at the heart of the potato's Andean origins.

In the wake of spiralling food prices, the conference looked at ways of increasing the potato's role in food production, especially in poor economies. As a crop, the potato has huge potential because it produces more food on less land than the major staples corn, wheat or rice.

One conference event that piqued my curiosity as a cook was a visit to a 12,000 hectare "Potato Park" near Cuzco, where farmers and researchers grow and study more than 600 traditional Andean potato varieties.

Here's a brief guide to some of the many currently available varieties:

Royal blue – waxy and yellow-fleshed – is excellent roasted with olive oil and rosemary or boiled whole and served.

Bintje – long and thin in shape with light-yellow flesh – is the perfect salad potato.

Desiree – round with light-yellow flesh and in most supermarkets – is a good all-rounder. Also good for gnocchi.

King Edward – long and oval with white-pink flesh – is very good baked or roasted.

Kipfler – long, cigar-shaped with light-yellow flesh, a rich creamy texture and great flavour – is best boiled for a salad or roasted.

Pinkeye – round with pink-blue "eyes" and rich, sweet golden flesh – is good for mash or a salad, as well as a casserole or curry.

Pontiac – round and white-fleshed – is excellent for mashing, roasting or frying.

Stewed potatoes

INGREDIENTS

1kg potatoes (sebago, spunta or toolangi delight)

3 tbsp extra virgin olive oil

4 Roma tomatoes (canned or fresh), pureed

2 garlic cloves, minced

1 tbsp finely chopped fresh rosemary

1 tbsp finely chopped fresh sage

½ cup chicken stock

METHOD

🍽 This dish breaks the rule by using floury potatoes in a relatively long, slow casserole.

🍽 Peel and dice a kilo of sebago, spunta or toolangi delight, cutting them about 3cm square. Heat extra virgin olive oil in a large pot over a medium flame. Add the potatoes, as well as pureed Roma tomatoes and stir. Now add minced garlic cloves, finely chopped fresh rosemary and fresh sage. Season and mix well. Pour in chicken stock.

🍽 Simmer over low heat, partially covered, for about 40 minutes, stirring occasionally until tender. Adjust the seasoning before serving.

Serves 6

What to look for

Avoid potatoes that have a green tinge – they've been exposed for a prolonged period to light, developing the toxin solanine. Choose firm potatoes that haven't sprouted and aren't bruised. Don't worry about dirt or mud; it protects the potato from bruising green. Remember to select the right potatoes for the dish being prepared.

Potatoes go with

Extra virgin olive oil; butter; milk and cream; herbs, such as rosemary, sage, parsley, coriander, thyme and chives; spices, especially cumin, coriander seed, paprika, saffron, cayenne and black pepper; mayonnaise; cream; cheeses such as gruyere and parmesan; salad leaves; vinegars; beef; lamb; chicken; fish; sausages; mushrooms; spinach; onions.

Perfect roast potatoes with rosemary

INGREDIENTS

2kg potatoes
¼ cup extra virgin olive oil
2 sprigs fresh rosemary
salt and pepper

METHOD

🍴 Peel potatoes (desiree are very good for roasting) and cut them into bite-sized pieces. Place them in a baking tray – use two trays if necessary so they aren't piled on top of each other – and sprinkle generously with extra virgin olive oil. Break up a couple of large sprigs of rosemary and add them to the potatoes. Season well with salt and toss them so they are completely coated in oil.

🍴 Roast in an oven preheated to 220C for about 35-40 minutes. Using a spatula, carefully turn the potatoes every 15 minutes so they are crisp and golden on all sides.

Serves 8 with roasted meats

Potato and apple frittata

INGREDIENTS

400g waxy potatoes, peeled and sliced very thin
4 tbsp clarified butter (ghee)
2 granny smith apples
4 large eggs
80g parmesan, grated
2 pinches salt
freshly cracked pepper

METHOD

🍴 Pat the potatoes dry after peeling and slicing. Melt the butter in a wide pan and distribute the potatoes evenly. It doesn't matter if they are on top of one another. Cook on a medium-low heat for about 30 minutes, shaking the pan every now and then so they don't stick.

🍴 Peel the apples, cut them into quarters and remove the cores. Distribute them on top of the potatoes and continue cooking for another 20 minutes.

🍴 Beat the eggs and parmesan together in a bowl with a couple of pinches of salt and a little freshly cracked pepper. Distribute the egg mixture over the potatoes and apples and turn up the flame.

🍴 Turn the frittata once to cook on the other side. Serve hot.

Serves 4-6

STRAWBERRIES

The punnets of strawberries in our fruit shops fall steadily in price in seemingly inverse proportion to their intensifying aroma as spring marches on. Anyone who has strawberries growing in their backyard will notice the increasing number of ripe fruits on the ever-widening reach of the plant's runners.

Dig out your favourite jam recipes because spring is when strawberries are both inexpensive and plentiful. While it's a bit of a chore, the strawberry jam made now will be enjoyed many times over the coming year, especially during the colder months.

A favourite around my place is strawberry and rhubarb compote. It keeps well in the refrigerator and can be used to accompany icecream, yoghurt, muesli or simply spread on toast or scones. It's excellent layered with cream in a sponge cake or with honey or vanilla panna cotta.

Strawberries are particularly good with pastry. Sugared or caramelised puff pastry, thick vanilla custard and strawberries are a great combination. Or try encasing strawberries that have been halved and rolled generously in sugar in buttered filo and then baked in the oven.

The French like to add strawberries to red wine. It's an unusual combination that works very well as long as the wine used is medium bodied. Another strange-but-inspired combination is to dust strawberries with a little sugar and to sprinkle with balsamic vinegar, the older the vinegar the better. Leave for half an hour (mixing gently every so often), and then serve with some cream or gelato.

Strawberry and rhubarb compote

INGREDIENTS

6 rhubarb stalks
200g sugar
1 tsp vanilla essence
2 tbsp water
1.5kg strawberries
3 cloves
1 small cinnamon stick

METHOD

- Cut rhubarb stalks into 3cm lengths and simmer with sugar, vanilla essence and water till the rhubarb pieces soften. This should take about 10 minutes, depending on the thickness of the rhubarb stalks.
- Add 1kg of the strawberries (cut in quarters) with cloves and cinnamon stick. Simmer for another 10 minutes. Remove from the heat, add remaining 500g strawberries (again cut into quarters), mix well and allow the mixture to cool. Store in a sealed container in the refrigerator till needed.

Makes about 2 litres compote

What to look for

Let your nose guide you. Look for fruit that is well coloured and glossy — any softness on the berry or blemish should be avoided. Turn the punnet over. If there is any "weeping" or "bleeding" the strawberries are probably past their use-by date and good only for jam. While there are many varieties of strawberry planted in Queensland, chances are the camarosa is the one you'll be buying till the season finishes around Melbourne Cup Day. My local fruiterer loves this variety because it produces big, luscious fruit that is every bit as flavoursome as it looks. The camarosa also keeps well and its flesh is deep red all the way through to the middle.

Strawberries go with

Cream; creme fraiche; yoghurt; mascarpone; honey; lemon juice; pastry; butter; vinegar; brandy and armagnac; kirsch; port; muscat; tokay; and, of course, champagne.

Strawberries with orange-flower water

Strawberries with balsamic vinegar

INGREDIENTS

600g strawberries

1 tbsp balsamic vinegar (best quality you can afford)

3 tbsp caster sugar

METHOD

🍽 Wash and dry the strawberries. Trim and quarter them into a bowl. Add the balsamic vinegar and mix them gently with a spoon taking care not to bruise them. Let them macerate for 10 minutes and add the sugar.

🍽 Once again, carefully mix them with a spoon. Leave them another 10 minutes and then they are ready to serve.

🍽 Spoon the strawberries, along with some of the juice, onto scoops of vanilla gelato.

Serves 4-6

INGREDIENTS

2 punnets strawberries

1 tsp red wine vinegar

50g caster sugar

200ml freshly squeezed orange juice

50ml orange-flower water

METHOD

🍽 This dish is adapted from a recipe by Joel Robuchon.

🍽 Gently wash strawberries, then quarter them and put them in a bowl. Add red wine vinegar and caster sugar. Mix gently and leave for an hour, covered, in the fridge to marinate.

🍽 Meanwhile, prepare a mixture of the freshly squeezed orange juice and the orange-flower water. After an hour, add the mixture to the marinated strawberries, chill well then serve with some candied orange peel on top.

Serves 4

CHIVES

From the large allium family come some of the most useful and flavoursome ingredients in cooking. Onion, leek, garlic and shallot are among the more common members of this 1250 species family but there are many others that play smaller, subtler roles in a dish.

Chives are mostly bit-players, destined never to star, but their particular flavour – a subtle blend of mild garlic and onion – has ensured that some classic dishes need them to succeed.

Eggs of all types, not just hen, are wonderful with chives. The recipe below with salmon eggs is a case in point. It is an adaptation of a dish by Italian chef Gualtiero Marchesi. He uses caviar – sturgeon eggs – instead of salmon. But everyday, simple scrambled eggs also benefit from finely chopped chives, as do poached, fried or coddled eggs.

The French word for chives – *cive* – was used to name the medieval sauce 'civy', made by boiling the entrails of a pig with herbs – predominantly chives – and spices. For some reason the preparation has all but disappeared from modern cooking repertoires.

A dish that is still around and thriving is civet, also of medieval origin. Nowadays it refers to a sort of game stew made with wine and thickened with the animal's blood. Hare, venison and duck are commonly prepared this way. Back in the early middle ages, it was made using stewed meat (or a combination of meats) and served with bread soaked in wine and flavoured with onions or chives.

Prosciutto stuffed with ricotta, chives and leek

INGREDIENTS

1 large leek, washed and trimmed, cut into thin rounds
2 tbsp extra virgin olive oil
6 tbsp finely sliced chives
4 tbsp fresh ricotta
4 tbsp grated parmesan
pinch nutmeg
salt and pepper
8 thin slices prosciutto

METHOD

🍽 Heat the olive oil in a pan and lightly fry the leeks for 3-4 minutes until they are soft and sweet. Place in a bowl with the ricotta, chives, parmesan and nutmeg. Add a pinch or two of salt and a couple of turns of pepper. Mix well. Roll a tablespoon of the resulting mixture in each prosciutto slice and place the stuffed prosciutto on an oiled baking tray. Bake in a preheated 150C oven for 15 minutes.
Serves 4

Crab fritters

INGREDIENTS

100g very dry ricotta
100g breadcrumbs
100g crab meat
100g chopped green olives
1 whole egg
2 egg yolks
½ cup finely sliced chives
salt and pepper
plain flour
100ml extra virgin olive oil

METHOD

🍽 Mix the ricotta, breadcrumbs, crab, olives, eggs and egg yolks, and chives together in a bowl. Make sure the mixture is seasoned well with salt and pepper. Roll each into a ball about the diameter of a 50 cent piece. Roll lightly in the flour and fry in the olive oil till golden. Serve hot as a snack.
Serves 8

What to look for
Garlic chives are preferred in Asian cooking. They have a broad leaf rather than round and a much more pronounced garlic flavour. The Chinese use these in red-cooked dishes, soups, dumplings and of course, their famous pancakes.
Flowering chives have small yellow buds at their ends and hollow, tender stems. They are considered a delicacy in many Asian cuisines and stir-fried on their own with a little light soy.

Chives go with
Eggs; rice; pasta; fish and shellfish; crustaceans; onions; garlic; potatoes; cucumber; tomato; beetroot (boiled and roasted); mayonnaise.

Spaghettini with chives and salmon eggs

INGREDIENTS

240g spaghettini (thin spaghetti)

4 tbsp extra virgin olive oil

$\frac{1}{3}$ cup finely sliced chives

160g salmon roe (eggs)

salt to taste

METHOD

🍽 This is a very simple dish and, as such, it relies on the quality of the ingredients for its ultimate success. Use the best extra virgin olive oil that can be afforded and artisan, bronze extruded pasta such as Giovanni Fabbri, Giuseppe Cocco or Martelli.

🍽 Bring a pot with abundant salted water to a rolling boil and plunge in the spaghettini. Cook till the pasta is al dente, drain and dress in a bowl with the olive oil. Mix well and allow to come to room temperature. Season with a little salt to taste and mix through the chives. Distribute among four plates and finish with some salmon roe on each.

Serves 4

EGGS

Perhaps the most apposite symbol of spring is the egg. Alan Davidson, in *The Penguin Companion to Food*, calls the egg "the astonishing and unintentional gift from birds to human beings, the acme of food packaging and a prime resource of occidental and oriental cooks alike. It is also the highest measure of ignorance and incompetence in the kitchen: 'He/she can't even boil an egg.'"

Long ago the egg became central to fertility festivals such as Easter, symbolising new life and rebirth. In Chinese mythology the universe is egg-shaped, the yolk is the earth and the white albumen is the heavens.

In the cook's universe, the egg is the essential binding ingredient. It traps air, liquid and fat. It sets when heated, though because of the different kinds of proteins in the white and yolk, each part behaves differently when cooked. At lower temperatures, the white makes meringue and souffle light and fluffy. At higher temperatures the yolk produces silky-smooth custard and light-as-air zabaglione. Indeed, without the egg, many of the things we whip up in the kitchen would not be possible.

Eggs go with
Butter and extra virgin olive oil; cream; cheese; herbs; soy sauce; bacon; prosciutto; sausages; tomatoes; avocado; asparagus; garlic; onions; chives; mushrooms; spinach; smoked salmon; crab; prawns; yabbies; crayfish; bread; mayonnaise and hollandaise.

Rich runny custard

INGREDIENTS

200g sugar
12 egg yolks
1 litre fresh cream
1 tsp vanilla essence

METHOD

🍽 Whisk sugar with egg yolks until the mixture turns pale and creamy. Heat fresh cream until almost at the boil. Add slowly to the egg mixture while whisking well, then return to the saucepan. On a medium-low heat, stir constantly until the custard thickens and coats the back of a spoon. Transfer to a bowl, add vanilla essence and allow the hot custard to cool to room temperature before refrigerating.

🍽 Add to cakes, Christmas puddings and panettone. Keeps for a week in the refrigerator.

Serves 12

Broad bean cocotte

INGREDIENTS

1 cup broad beans, unshelled
2 tbsp extra virgin olive oil
8 eggs
8 tbsp cream
80g parmesan, grated
salt and pepper

METHOD

🍽 Cocotte is a French term for the ramekins used to cook the dish. Any small shallow ceramic dishes can be used.

🍽 Double peel the broad beans by removing them from their pods first and then from their individual shells. Bring a pot of salted water to the boil and blanch the broad beans for 30 seconds.

🍽 Preheat the oven to 180C. Line four ceramic dishes with the olive oil and break two eggs into each. Add 2 tablespoons of cream to each and arrange the broad beans on top. Sprinkle the parmesan evenly across the four dishes and season with salt and pepper. Place in the oven for 10-15 minutes till the eggs have cooked but the yolks are still runny.

Serves 4

Spring herb and rocket frittata

INGREDIENTS

8 large eggs

½ cup chopped fresh herbs (chives, parsley, tarragon, chervil and
   thyme)

1 cup roughly chopped rocket

½ cup grated parmesan

salt and pepper

1 tbsp extra virgin olive oil

METHOD

Crack eggs into a bowl. Beat lightly, then add chopped fresh herbs, rocket leaves and grated parmesan. Season with salt and pepper and mix well.

Heat extra virgin olive oil in a 20cm iron skillet until it starts to smoke. Add the egg mixture. As it cooks, repeatedly lift the edges with a spatula so the raw mixture fills the space. This will trap air and make the frittata light and fluffy. Turn the frittata onto a plate, slide it uncooked side first back into the pan and finish cooking for 2-3 minutes.

Makes 20cm frittata

BLOOD ORANGES

Go into any bar in Italy in late winter through to early spring and ask for a fresh orange juice. More often than not you'll be rewarded with a glass of shining, blood red liquid. For the uninitiated it can be quite confronting; it looks nothing like orange juice apart from its liquid state. But taste it and you'll remember that flavour forever.

There was a period early last century when blood oranges were grown in Australia but by the 1920s the trees were pulled up. I've spoken with some of the old timers at the Sydney Produce Markets and they reckon blood oranges didn't catch on because of their strange looks.

Blood orange skin is flecked with colours ranging from rust to scarlet and even garnet and purple. The sanguine juice is unmistakably citrus in flavour but with a raspberry aftertaste. It's not quite as sweet as the navel orange and the size of the fruit is almost always small.

The simplest of all preparations is adding the segments to a composed salad and then incorporating some of the juice into the dressing. Blood orange marries particularly well with fennel (still in great condition) and good olive oil. Because the juice is not too sweet, cooked crustaceans like prawns, crayfish or yabbies are good as the centrepiece.

Blood orange's intense colour and flavour make stunning compote, especially with the addition of some of its peel. Add segments to custard or frangipane tarts and then glaze with blood orange jelly. Of course, the easiest way to enjoy them is to do as the Italians and simply squeeze a big glass full and drink it.

Blood orange jelly

INGREDIENTS

1.5 litres freshly squeezed blood orange juice

500g sugar

5 sheets of titanium strength gelatine (5g each) or equivalent powder*

1 blood orange, well washed

* Titanium strength gelatine is available in good kitchen supply shops.

METHOD

- This recipe is based on a traditional Sicilian preparation.
- Once squeezed, strain the blood orange juice through a couple of layers of cheesecloth. Put the juice in a stainless steel saucepan with the sugar and bring to the boil. Turn it off and stir until all the sugar has dissolved.
- If using sheet gelatine, place it in a bowl of water to soften for a few minutes. Remove and give the gelatine a good squeeze. Whisk it into the warm blood orange and sugar mixture to dissolve fully. Let it cool a little more and place into one large glass serving bowl or eight smaller individual ones.
- Slice the remaining blood orange into wedges, remove any seeds and distribute into the setting jelly.
- Place in the refrigerator, covered, overnight.

Serves 8

Blood oranges go with

Cream; sugar; honey; chocolate; sponge cake; pastry, especially sweet shortcrust, puff and choux; onion; fennel; strawberries; mint; crustaceans such as crab, prawns and lobster; extra virgin olive oil; red wine vinegar; rocket; lamb's lettuce (mâche); almonds; macadamia; grappa; Campari.

Blood orange, fennel and prawn salad

Blood orange puddings

INGREDIENTS

6 blood oranges

3 fennel bulbs

24 cooked king prawns, peeled and deveined

6 tbsp extra virgin olive oil

2 tbsp red wine vinegar

salt and pepper

METHOD

🍽 Slice the skin and pith right off each orange to reveal the red flesh, and then cut the individual segments into a bowl. Squeeze any remaining juice left in the orange carcass into another bowl.

🍽 Trim off the first two or three tough outer layers of the fennel bulbs and keep some of the green fronds that are attached to their stems. Finely slice each fennel bulb and place the slices on one large serving plate or six individual ones.

🍽 Place the prawns and blood orange segments neatly on top. Mix the blood orange juice, vinegar and oil together with a little salt and pepper.

🍽 Dress the salad with this mixture and finish by sprinkling some of the fennel fronds.

Serves 6

INGREDIENTS

250g unsalted butter

1 cup sugar

1 tsp vanilla essence

4 eggs

2 cups plain flour

2¼ tsp baking powder

pinch salt

¾ cup milk

zest of 2 blood oranges, finely grated

500ml blood orange juice

400g sugar

METHOD

🍽 Cream the butter and cup of sugar. Add the vanilla, two whole eggs and two yolks, reserving the two whites. Sift the flour, baking powder and salt together, then add to the mixture. Mix in the milk and the zest. Whisk the remaining two egg whites and fold into the mixture.

🍽 Butter and sugar dariole or pudding moulds and fill them with the mixture. Bake in a bain marie (water bath) in a preheated 180C oven for 30 minutes – pierce with a skewer to test; skewer should be dry when extracted. While puddings are in the oven, bring the blood orange juice and 400g sugar to the boil, then remove from heat.

🍽 Once out of the oven and still hot, prick the surface of the puddings and pour some of the syrup into each one. Allow to cool a little, turn out and serve.

Makes 8 puddings

SPRING ASPARAGUS

Asparagus season begins late in August with produce arriving from south-eastern Queensland, then Mildura. As the weather gets warmer, the big crop from Victoria kicks in and, when the shop price hits $1 a bunch, the season is at its peak. That's when asparagus should be used all over the menu.

As a dish on its own, asparagus works well with soft-poached, fried or scrambled eggs. Lightly blanched and chopped, it can even feature in a frittata or omelette.

If the spears are thick, plunge them into rapidly boiling, salted water for a minute – less if they're thin. Serve them hot with bubbling, nut-brown butter and grated parmesan as a first course.

Fresh, crisp asparagus is good raw, added to a salad with spicy rocket, bitter radicchio or tangy watercress and tossed with your favourite dressing.

Similarly, it can be blanched in boiling water, drained and plunged into iced water before drying well and adding to a salad.

If you prefer simpler pleasures, dress the cooked asparagus with the best extra virgin olive oil available and season with salt and freshly cracked pepper.

Green asparagus is the most commonly available type but there are also purple and highly prized white varieties that are well worth seeking out.

Green and purple asparagus don't need to be peeled as long as the tough stem-ends are cut off. The white tends to have firmer skin and its stem is peeled to just under the head before cooking.

Asparagus with poached eggs

INGREDIENTS

500g asparagus spears, trimmed
4 eggs
2 tbsp white wine vinegar
4 tbsp extra virgin olive oil
80g parmesan, shaved thin
salt and pepper

METHOD

- Plunge the asparagus spears into rapidly boiling water for 60 seconds, drain and distribute them onto one large or four individual serving plates.
- Poach the eggs in simmering water with the vinegar until they are set but still have soft and runny yolks. Place one egg on each of the serves of asparagus, dress with the olive oil, season and add the shaved parmesan. The soft yolk will provide a delicious sauce for the dish.

Serves 4

Asparagus with boiled egg salsa

INGREDIENTS

2 eggs
1 tbsp chives, finely sliced
1 tbsp mustard
salt and pepper
2 tbsp boiling water
200ml extra virgin olive oil, not too peppery
1 tbsp red wine vinegar
600g asparagus, the thicker the better, trimmed from their woody ends

METHOD

- Make the salsa first by boiling the eggs for 7 minutes. Cool a little by placing them under cold running water for a minute. Peel and separate the firm yolk from the white. Chop the whites into fine dice. Place the yolks in a bowl and add the chives, mustard, salt and pepper to taste, and boiling water. Mix well to form a paste, then add the olive oil and whisk well. Add the vinegar and the chopped egg whites and fold through.
- Plunge the trimmed asparagus into plenty of salted, boiling water for 3-5 minutes, depending on thickness.
- Serve hot or cold dressed with the salsa.

Serves 4

Spring asparagus goes with
Butter; cream; mayonnaise; extra virgin olive oil; cheeses, especially parmesan, asiago, fontina, gruyere, raclette and manchego; mustard; olives; capers; chives; sage; parsley; thyme; leek; zucchini; potato; lemon; prosciutto and speck; egg; rice, noodles and pasta; anchovies; most shellfish, especially scallops, prawn and lobster; smoked salmon and trout.

Macaroni cheese with asparagus

INGREDIENTS

500g macaroni pasta

3 bunches asparagus

150g gruyere or sharp cheddar, grated

150g parmesan, grated

100g salted butter

freshly cracked pepper

METHOD

Bring a pot of water to the boil for the pasta. Meanwhile, trim 1cm from the base ends of the asparagus, then cut the spears into 3cm lengths. A minute before the pasta is ready, add the asparagus pieces to the water. Drain and put immediately into a large saucepan, on low heat, with the cheese, butter and pepper. Stir well until the macaroni is creamy and totally coated with the cheese. Serve straight away.

Serves 6-8

SPRING PEAS

Fresh peas are a genuine seasonal treat. They taste better in spring – they're sweeter, more tender and flavoursome. Although modern freezing, canning and packaging have provided convenience in terms of time saved, the price has been loss of flavour. As Stephanie Alexander notes in *The Cook's Companion*: "Frozen peas mimic the taste of freshly picked, quickly cooked green peas but, as so few members of the public seem to be interested or prepared to grow or pod fresh peas, the flavour of the frozen product has become the standard."

Once peas are plucked, the sugars convert to starch relatively quickly, so they should be cooked as soon as possible. If not, rather than being soft, sweet and succulent, they will be firm and mealy and have to be cooked a long time before they soften. I would encourage anyone with a garden or planter boxes to grow peas simply for the pleasure of eating them in spring.

The pods should look bright and waxy, and the peas inside not too large (an indication they have been in the ground too long). To prepare them, bring salted water to a rolling boil, drop in the peas for 4-5 minutes, then drain well. If saving them for later or using as part of a salad, plunge them in ice water for 30 seconds. If serving them hot, toss with butter or extra virgin olive oil, season with pepper and serve with shaved parmesan or sheep's milk cheese, parsley and mint.

Chicken with peas and chilli

INGREDIENTS

800g chicken thighs, boneless and skin off
3 tbsp extra virgin olive oil
1 medium onion, peeled and diced
2 cloves garlic, minced
2 rashers of prosciutto, cut into thin strips
2 red chillies, sliced
4 stems fresh thyme
1 punnet cherry tomatoes, each sliced in half
300g shelled peas, cooked
salt and pepper

METHOD

🍽 Cut the chicken thighs into bite-sized pieces. Heat the olive oil in a pan and lightly fry the onion, garlic, prosciutto and chilli for 2 minutes. Turn up the heat, add the chicken and the thyme and fry for 3-4 minutes, constantly stirring. Add the cherry tomatoes and the peas.

🍽 Season and simmer for 5 minutes. Turn off the heat and rest for another 5 minutes. Serve with rice or couscous.

Serves 4-6

Florentine peas

INGREDIENTS

2 tbsp extra virgin olive oil
80g pancetta, sliced in short strips
600g shelled peas
1 garlic clove, peeled and finely sliced
1 litre (or a little more) chicken broth
handful flat-leaf parsley, roughly chopped
salt and pepper

METHOD

🍽 Heat the olive oil in a pot and lightly fry the pancetta for 2-3 minutes, making sure it doesn't colour too much.

🍽 Add the shelled peas and garlic as well as the chicken broth. The peas should be covered by the broth, if not add a little more. Bring to a simmer, place a lid on the pot and turn down low to cook for about 20 minutes.

🍽 Remove the lid, add the parsley and season with salt and pepper. Stir well and simmer a couple more minutes.

🍽 Remove and rest until the peas are warm. Serve with braised meat or fish.

Serves 6

Spring peas go with

Butter; extra virgin olive oil; chicken; veal; slow-cooked dishes such as braised beef cheek and pork belly; smoked ham, bacon and prosciutto; onions; leeks; garlic; parsley; mint; sage; coriander; scallops; crab; prawns; carrots; chickpeas; pasta; rice; risotto.

Grilled veal cutlet with spring pea puree

INGREDIENTS

4 tbsp extra virgin olive oil

4 veal cutlets

salt and pepper

400g shelled peas

50g butter

METHOD

🍽 Heat 1 tablespoon of the olive oil on a flat grill or frypan. Fry the cutlets for 2-3 minutes on each side, depending on the thickness, on a medium heat. Season with salt and pepper, turn off heat and allow the cutlets to rest in the pan.

🍽 Cook the peas in plenty of salted boiling water for a few minutes until tender. Drain and puree in a food processor while hot with the butter and the remaining 3 tablespoons of olive oil. Season and serve with the veal cutlet. Also good with grilled or barbecued beef or fish.

Serves 4

EXTRA VIRGIN OLIVE OIL

When it comes to oil, I have a preference for extra virgin olive oil. Whether it's for cooking, dipping or dressing, no other oil will do. There are still some people who advise against cooking with this oil because, they say, it burns easily. Its high smoking-point is 210C, well above the ideal frying temperature of 180C.

But it must be extra virgin, the unadulterated oil from pressed olives. At home, you'll benefit from having two or three different olive oils. The first is an all-round cheaper one for frying fish, rubbing on a lamb leg before roasting, tossing through vegetables before baking and frying chips.

Next you'll need an estate grown, light- to medium-bodied oil for dressing delicate seafood salads and vegetables or even dipping your bread into. The third oil should be robust and peppery, able to stand up to big flavours. Use this oil raw as well, drizzled over oxtail and barley soup or mixed with mashed roast garlic and anchovy then spread over good bread as a base for a corned beef or roast lamb sandwich.

Extra virgin olive oil goes with

All meats, especially roasts; carpaccio (raw, thinly sliced) tuna, swordfish, beef and yearling beef; raw vegetables, especially fennel, carrot, celery heart, radish, tomato; fresh cheeses such as mozzarella; aged cheeses such as pecorino and parmesan; all salad leaves; cooked vegetables such as artichoke, spinach, mushrooms and beans; eggs, especially soft-boiled and runny.

Rhubarb, cucumber and rocket salad

INGREDIENTS

3-4 young rhubarb stalks
1-2 cucumbers
2 tbsp coarse salt
bunch rocket leaves, washed and chopped
2 tbsp lemon juice
4 tbsp extra virgin olive oil
salt and pepper
handful chopped mint

METHOD

- This Iranian salad is adapted from a recipe by Paula Wolfert.
- Wash rhubarb stalks and strip away any tough outer membrane. Peel cucumbers. Slice the vegetables finely at an angle and toss in a bowl with coarse salt. Let stand for 10 minutes, rinse, drain and pat dry.
- In a salad bowl place rocket leaves (not wild rocket – it has little flavour) with the cucumber and rhubarb. Dress with lemon juice and extra virgin olive oil. Season with salt and pepper to taste and garnish with a good handful of chopped mint leaves.

Serves 4

Spiedini (skewers) of prawns, scallops and cherry tomatoes

INGREDIENTS

6 skewers
36 cherry tomatoes
6 green king prawns, peeled, deveined and each cut into three pieces
12 scallops
2 cloves garlic, minced
handful flat-leaf parsley, roughly chopped
handful oregano, roughly chopped
juice of 1 lemon
½ cup extra virgin olive oil
2 tbsp extra virgin olive oil, for grilling or frying

METHOD

- On each skewer, start with a cherry tomato, then a piece of prawn, tomato, scallop, tomato, piece of prawn, tomato, scallop, tomato, piece of prawn and finally a tomato. Lay the finished spiedini on a plate and refrigerate.
- In a bowl, mix the garlic, parsley, oregano, lemon juice and olive oil together. Just before cooking, remove the skewers from the refrigerator and brush with the olive oil mixture. Prepare a grill (or a large frypan) by heating 2 tablespoons of extra virgin olive oil.
- Grill the spiedini on both sides. Serve with some more of the olive oil mixture spooned on top.

Serves 6

Ocean trout poached in extra virgin olive oil

INGREDIENTS

4 x 160g ocean trout pieces,
   skinned
2½ cups olive oil
4 cloves garlic, sliced
sprig of thyme
salt and pepper

METHOD

🍽 Lightly salt pieces of skinned ocean trout and refrigerate for an hour. In a frypan wide enough to fit the fish pieces comfortably, add olive oil, garlic and thyme. Simmer gently until the garlic is lightly golden, turn off the heat and discard the garlic and thyme. Remove the fish pieces from the fridge, pat them dry and leave out for about 10 minutes to reach room temperature.

🍽 Using a thermometer (and a low flame) bring the pan of oil up to 70C. Add the fish pieces gently. If the fish is not completely covered, add more oil. Once the temperature reaches 70C turn off the heat and leave for 20 minutes.

🍽 Remove with a spatula, season with salt and pepper and serve with rhubarb, cucumber and rocket salad.

Serves 4

ONIONS

There are few smells that pique the appetite like onions gently frying in butter or olive oil. They are one of the essential building blocks of many dishes.

A lot of preparations begin with simmering onions. From tomato sauce to slow-braised beef, onions provide a base, a background, on which layers of other flavours are built. Stocks and broths rely on the aromatic onion for balance, and soups are less satisfying without it.

But onions are also stars in their own right. Spanish or red onions are generally milder than white or brown varieties and are ideal raw and thinly sliced in a Thai beef salad or tossed with wedges of ripe tomato and dressed with extra virgin olive oil and vinegar. A little finely chopped raw onion is excellent folded through mashed potato.

Unpeeled, sliced in half and sprinkled with olive oil, a little paprika, salt and pepper and fennel seeds, onions can be barbecued until they lose their crunch and concentrate their sweetness.

Alternatively, peeled and cut into wedges, onions can be tossed in olive oil, salt and pepper and roasted in an oven for 15 minutes. While still hot, sprinkle them with a little balsamic vinegar to create a perfect accompaniment to grilled beef or fish.

Onion confit

INGREDIENTS

2 tbsp olive oil

12 cups thinly sliced white or
   brown onions

1 tsp salt

½ tsp freshly ground black
   pepper

1 cup chicken stock

2 tbsp white wine vinegar

2 tbsp fresh thyme

4 anchovy fillets, chopped
   (optional)

METHOD

- This is a recipe from *Think Like a Chef* by American chef Tom Colicchio.
- Heat olive oil in a large, deep skillet until it slides easily across the pan. Add thinly sliced white or brown onions, salt and freshly ground black pepper. Reduce heat to medium-low and simmer, stirring occasionally, until the onions are soft but not brown – about 30 minutes. Add chicken stock and white wine vinegar, simmering until the pan is dry and the onions golden – about 30 minutes more. Add fresh thyme and anchovy fillets (optional), adjust seasoning and mix well. Use warm or at room temperature.

Serves 6

Onions go with

Butter; extra virgin olive oil; cream; vinegar; rice; pasta; bread, especially toast; all meat; bacon, pancetta, speck and prosciutto; all fish and shellfish; most vegetables, especially garlic; capsicum, eggplant, tomato, potato and zucchini; cos; iceberg; rocket; sorrel; radicchio; herbs such as basil, thyme, tarragon, rosemary and oregano; fresh and soft cheeses such as mozzarella, cottage, ricotta and goat's curd.

Onion and parmesan tart

Roast red onions stuffed with eggplant

INGREDIENTS

8 medium-large red onions, peeled

500g ripe tomatoes

350g eggplant

2 good pinches salt

4 tbsp extra virgin olive oil

2 shallots, peeled and very finely sliced

sprig of oregano

salt and pepper

METHOD

🍽 Plunge the peeled onions into a pot of salted, boiling water for 5 minutes. Remove and set aside. Plunge the tomatoes into the same water for 20 seconds, remove to a bowl of cold water. This will loosen the skin so it peels easily. Once peeled, cut the tomatoes into 1cm dice. Chop the eggplant into dice the same size. Toss them with a couple of good pinches of salt and leave for 30 minutes. Afterwards, pat them dry.

🍽 Heat the olive oil in a pan and lightly fry the sliced shallots for a minute. Add the tomato and eggplant dice as well as the oregano and fry, continually stirring, for 5-6 minutes. Season with salt and pepper and set aside.

🍽 Remove the centre of each of the onions, leaving only the very outer layer or two. Carefully stuff the onions with the mixture and lay them on an oiled baking tray. Preheat the oven to 200C and roast for 35-45 minutes.

Serves 4

INGREDIENTS

savoury shortcrust pastry

4 or 5 medium white or brown onions

½ cup grated parmesan

salt and freshly ground pepper

METHOD

🍽 Line a 27cm tart tin with savoury shortcrust pastry dough. Refrigerate until needed. Preheat the oven to 220C. Peel and slice white or brown onions. Place them in a bowl and toss with freshly grated parmesan and a little salt and freshly ground pepper.

🍽 Fill the tart shell evenly with the onion mixture and bake for about 15-20 minutes until the topmost onions have caramelised. Serve hot or at room temperature.

Makes 27cm tart

PARSLEY

There are many essential kitchen herbs. Mostly, these herbs are kept specially for certain dishes – rosemary with roast lamb; sage with pork; thyme with mussels; tarragon with salmon; coriander with black beans, and so on. But, for me, parsley is the one truly indispensable herb. I use it daily and in so many dishes that I would be at a loss without it.

One of the simplest ways of demonstrating parsley's easygoing nature is to chop a cupful of its leaves, along with two or three cloves of garlic. Blanch about 250g of topped and tailed green beans so they're soft but not overcooked. Drain them and, while they're still warm, toss them with the parsley and garlic then dress with 4 tablespoons of extra virgin olive oil and season with salt. Let the beans cool a little before serving, as they'll be much tastier.

Parsley goes with
Fish, especially grilled, barbecued or smoked; garlic; butter; extra virgin olive oil; lemon juice; salads; cheese; cold-roasted or poached meats; green beans; peas; soy beans; broad beans; chickpeas; lentils; leeks and onions; artichokes; zucchini; roast tomatoes; eggs; grilled and braised mushrooms; long pasta such as spaghetti and linguini; marinades.

Tartare sauce

INGREDIENTS

4 eggs
½ onion, finely chopped
½ cup chopped flat-leaf parsley
200ml extra virgin olive oil
4 tbsp white wine vinegar
1 tbsp fresh chopped tarragon
salt and pepper

METHOD

🍽 Hard boil three of the eggs. Remove the shells and cut the eggs in half and scoop out the yolks and place in a bowl. Add the raw yolk of the fourth egg to the cooked yolks and mash until smooth. Mix in finely chopped onion and chopped flat-leaf parsley. Whisk in 50ml of extra virgin olive oil, a few drops at a time, as you would if making mayonnaise. Once the mixture has thickened, mix in a tablespoon of the white wine vinegar. Repeat this process until a total of 200ml of olive oil and 4 tablespoons of vinegar have been added to the mixture. Add tarragon and season with salt and pepper to taste.

🍽 This sauce is the perfect accompaniment to poached or battered fish and cold meats.

Serves 10

Pan-fried barramundi with salsa verde

Tuna, green bean and parsley salad

INGREDIENTS

500g green beans, topped and tailed

250g tuna packed in extra virgin olive oil, crumbled and oil retained

juice of 1 lemon

handful flat-leaf parsley, chopped

4 dried tomatoes, chopped

3 tbsp extra virgin olive oil

salt and pepper

METHOD

 Cook the beans in plenty of salted boiling water for about 5 minutes. Drain and transfer them to a large bowl.

 Add the rest of the ingredients, including the drained oil and juice from the tuna, season with salt and pepper to taste and toss.

 Serve as part of an antipasto or as a snack with good bread.

Serves 4

INGREDIENTS

1 slice bread, crust removed

4 tbsp milk

1 egg, hard boiled and peeled

2 cups flat-leaf parsley

juice of 1 lemon

6 anchovies

3 garlic cloves, peeled

1 cup extra virgin olive oil

salt and pepper

2 tbsp capers

1 barramundi fillet

2 tbsp extra virgin olive oil, for frying

METHOD

 To make salsa verde, moisten a slice of bread, crust removed, with milk until it is completely absorbed. Place the bread, a hard-boiled egg, fresh flat-leaf parsley, the juice of a lemon, anchovies and garlic cloves into a food processor and turn it on. Slowly pour in extra virgin olive oil until it is well blended. Season with salt, mix in capers and store in a jar in the refrigerator until needed.

 Cut a barramundi fillet (or other large fish) into 70-80g pieces, leaving the skin on. Heat 2 tablespoons of extra virgin olive oil in a skillet until the oil begins to smoke. Salt the skin side of the barramundi pieces and fry on that side at moderate heat for 2 minutes. Turn and cook on the other side until just done.

 Serve with the salsa verde and salad or vegetables.

Serves 6

PASTA

There is more than the obvious difference between the pasta you make at home and the one you buy. The homemade variety is usually a combination of eggs and soft wheat flour (plain or Italian 00), which makes it easy to form dough and roll.

Hard or durum wheat pasta, usually bought in dried form, tends to keep a firmer texture (al dente) when cooked. It is made by mixing flour with water and extruding the paste through either Teflon or bronze dies to form almost any shape. Bronze-extruded pasta will almost always cost more because it is a slower process and is reserved for artisan-made brands.

When devising sauces, keep it simple and look for contrasts in flavour and colour. Remember that the pasta is not only a vehicle for the sauce but also an essential element of the dish. Treat it with respect and don't overcook it.

Pasta goes with
Butter; extra virgin olive oil; soups and broths; tomato; eggplant; beans; zucchini; chickpeas; chilli; garlic; most herbs, especially basil, oregano, parsley, sage, thyme and tarragon; mozzarella; parmesan; gruyere; feta; goat's cheese; chicken; veal; pork; rabbit; quail; hare.

Pasta with butter, parmesan and sage

INGREDIENTS
100ml olive oil
40 sage leaves
450g pasta
150g butter, thinly sliced
150g parmesan, freshly grated
salt and pepper

METHOD
- In a frypan, heat olive oil until it is just smoking. Fry sage leaves for 30 seconds or so until crisp. Remove and drain them on absorbent paper.
- Bring a large pot of salted water to a rapid boil. In a large bowl, place thinly sliced butter. Cook pasta in the water, drain and, while very hot, toss it in the bowl with the butter, adding grated parmesan cheese. The pasta should be creamy. Season with a little salt and pepper and serve immediately with the fried sage leaves.

Serves 4

Garlic and anchovy lasagne from Piemonte

INGREDIENTS
100g butter
8-10 anchovy fillets, drained and finely chopped
3 garlic cloves, finely minced
500g lasagna sheets, cut to about 3cm x 7cm
3-4 garlic cloves, finely minced
100g grated parmesan
freshly ground pepper

METHOD
- It's probably not what we would normally consider lasagna, but refers literally to the sheet used in this delicious combination of unlikely ingredients.
- Melt the butter slowly in a large enamel or non-stick pan over low heat, making sure it doesn't fry. Add the anchovies and garlic and warm them in the butter for 5 minutes, mashing them every now and then with a wooden spoon.
- Cook the pasta sheets in plenty of salted boiling water, drain well and toss in the pan (with the anchovies and garlic) with half the parmesan and lots of freshly grated pepper.
- Serve straight away, passing around the remaining parmesan for those who want more.

Serves 6

Make your own pasta

INGREDIENTS

eggs
plain flour

METHOD

 I have always found it easier to make pasta without a precise recipe because there are too many variables – the size of the eggs, the condition of the flour and even the humidity or lack thereof on the day. As a general rule, one egg to 100g of flour is standard. Think about how many people you are feeding and allow 150g of plain flour for each. Make a pile with the flour then form a wide well in the centre. Crack enough whole eggs into the crater and slowly bring the flour and egg together to make dough that is neither too sticky nor too wet. Wet dough is better initially because it is easier to add more flour to a wet mixture than it is to add more eggs to a dry mixture. If it is sticky, then simply add more flour. Once you have a cohesive lump, knead it continually by putting it through the rollers on the widest setting of your pasta machine. Roll through and fold in half then roll through again, repeating till you have smooth, silky dough. Now roll thinner with each pass-through then cut into the desired shape.

PIPIS

Up the beach, in the late afternoon as the tide receded, a group of people were doing what appeared to be a strange, tribal dance. As we got closer, it resembled a slow twist, feet disappearing into the sand and the wash. Up close, each had a bag slowly filling with pipis, dug out one by one from the soft, wet sand.

The pipi is a bivalve mollusc that likes to burrow at least 10cm below the intertidal sand on ocean beaches. Its strong, muscular "foot" is prime bait for most surf-dwelling fish and delicious eating for humans. Coastal Aborigines have harvested them for thousands of years.

Jennifer Isaacs describes how it's done in *Bush Food*: "The hunter must be a fast digger and have very sharp eyesight. As the tide turns and each wave laps the sand, pipis bury themselves deeper in the wet sand. They go vertically, leaving only a small hole or bubble ... and can descend 30cm in a couple of seconds."

(NSW Fisheries has ruled that, for health reasons, pipis may be collected legally on the state's beaches only for bait. Commercially fished pipis are perfectly safe to eat.)

Pipis go with
White and red wine; extra virgin olive oil; butter; roasted sesame oil; XO sauce; soy sauce; black beans; lemon and lime; fresh herbs, especially parsley, thyme, marjoram, coriander, sage, basil and oregano; fried pancetta and bacon; leeks; onions; garlic; shallots; spring onions; capsicum; chilli; potatoes.

Pirate's fish soup

INGREDIENTS

1 red capsicum, seeded and sliced
1 green capsicum, seeded and sliced
2 dried chillies, seeded and crumbled
4 garlic cloves, chopped
1 cup fresh herbs (thyme, basil, sage and chives)
200ml extra virgin olive oil
200ml red wine
300g medium octopus tentacles
300g cuttlefish, cleaned and cut into bit-sized tiles
300g de-bearded mussels
500g pipis
100ml white rum
salt and pepper

METHOD

- This recipe is adapted from *The Silver Spoon* by Phaidon Press.
- In a casserole dish put: red and green capsicums, dried chillies, chopped garlic cloves, fresh herbs, extra virgin olive oil and red wine. Cook over a medium heat for 10 minutes.
- Add medium octopus tentacles and cuttlefish and simmer for 20 minutes. Add de-bearded mussels, pipis and white rum. Mix well, cover and simmer for 5 minutes until the shells have opened.
- Season with salt and pepper to taste and serve.

Serves 6

Steamed pipis in wine with tomato and garlic

Fregola with pipis and saffron

INGREDIENTS

200g fregola Sarda (Sardinian couscous)

1 garlic clove, minced

4 tbsp extra virgin olive oil

400g pipis, washed

½ pinch saffron threads

½ cup chopped flat-leaf parsley

salt and pepper

METHOD

🍽 Fregola is the Italian version of couscous. If you can find the large Sardinian couscous, it is ideal for this dish.

🍽 Bring a pot of lightly salted water to the boil and cook the fregola as you would pasta so that it is still al dente.

🍽 Meanwhile, lightly fry the garlic in the olive oil so it becomes golden but not dark or burnt. Add the pipis and a ladle of the fregola cooking water to the pan with the garlic. Add the saffron, turn up the heat and cook until the pips have opened. Remove the pipis into a bowl and strain the cooking liquid through a double layer of muslin or a clean tea towel. Return the strained liquid to a clean pan. Remove the pipis from their shells and add the meat to the strained liquid.

🍽 Drain the fregola (keep a litre of the cooking water) and add it to the pan with the pipi meat. Add half the parsley and another ladle of the fregola cooking water. Add a good pinch of salt and simmer for 10-15 minutes, adding more fregola cooking water if necessary.

🍽 When cooked, season with salt and pepper to taste and serve with remaining parsley.

Serves 4

INGREDIENTS

3 garlic cloves, minced

2 tbsp extra virgin olive oil

1kg pipis, washed

2 ripe tomatoes, chopped

½ cup chopped flat-leaf parsley

2-3 red chillies, chopped (optional)

salt and pepper

1 cup dry white wine

METHOD

🍽 In a large pot with a lid, lightly fry minced garlic cloves in extra virgin olive oil for 30 seconds, making sure it doesn't brown. Add well-washed pipis, ripe tomatoes, flat-leaf parsley and red chillies (optional). Turn the heat right up, season with a little salt and pepper and give the pipis a good stir for a few seconds. Add dry white wine and place the lid on the pot. They should all open in 3-4 minutes. Check that they have; sometimes it's just a matter of giving the pot a good shake or stirring the pipis so they have room to open. Season with salt and pepper.

Serves 4

CHICKEN

Awhole roast chicken is one of the most appealing and pleasurable things to present to friends and family. It demands attention from all present lest the best parts be given to the most vocal.

The whole bird also leaves us with a carcass that can be put to good use. Place it in a large pot, cover with cold water and add chopped celery, onion and carrot. Bring to the boil then lower to a simmer for 3 hours. Strain, cool and refrigerate or freeze. The chicken stock can be used for countless things such as soup, risotto or sauces.

It's relatively simple for a competent cook to put together delicious dishes with great ingredients, but the mark of a really good cook is how cunningly the leftovers are used. It's not merely a case of thrift but also of time management. With a little planning the enormous amount of work put into one meal can pay off for days to come.

Chicken goes with
Extra virgin olive oil; butter; vinegar; prosciutto, pancetta and bacon; olives; anchovies; capers; all the alliums especially garlic; shallots, leeks and onions; most herbs; fennel; mustard; saffron; cumin; paprika; ginger; lemon and lime; chilli; mushrooms; tomatoes; root vegetables, especially potatoes, celeriac, carrots and parsnips; peas; capsicum; white and red wine.

Chicken with sage and spices

INGREDIENTS

2 tbsp plain flour

1 chicken weighing around 1.8 kilos, cut into 8 pieces

5 tbsp extra virgin olive oil

80g prosciutto, sliced thinly and cut into strips

125ml dry white wine

½ tsp ground mixed spice

8 large sage leaves

salt and pepper

METHOD

🍽 Flour the chicken pieces and fry in a pan with the olive oil till nicely golden – about 10 minutes. Add the sliced prosciutto and lightly fry for another minute. Add the white wine, the spice, the sage leaves and salt and pepper to taste. Mix well and place in a pre-heated 200C oven for 40 minutes until the chicken pieces are tender. Baste every 10 minutes or so. A few tablespoons of water may need to be added towards the end so that there is some sauce left.

🍽 Serve with grilled or roasted root vegetables.

Serves 4

Barbecued chicken with spring herbs and garlic

INGREDIENTS

2 small chickens or 4 spatchcocks

¼ cup each of parsley, tarragon, thyme and chives – finely chopped

3 garlic cloves, minced

4 tbsp extra virgin olive oil

salt and pepper

METHOD

🍽 Give each chicken a good wash and pat dry. Place a large, sharp knife in the cavity on one side of the backbone and slice through. Place the knife on the other side of the backbone and cut through, removing it entirely. (Follow the same method for spatchcocks. The spatchcock can now be flattened in one piece, ready for the barbecue.) Slice through each chicken at the breast end, giving four halves.

🍽 In a bowl, mix all the herbs together with the garlic. Coat each chicken with a little extra virgin olive oil and press the chopped herbs on each side of the four halves. Season with salt and pepper.

🍽 Place on the barbecue, skin side down. Turn and barbecue the other side, then serve with lemon wedges.

Serves 4

Roman-style chicken with capsicum

INGREDIENTS

1 2kg chicken

6 tbsp extra virgin olive oil

50g plain flour

1 onion, peeled and sliced

2 garlic cloves, minced

1 celery heart, thinly sliced

1 large red capsicum, seeded
  and cut into 1cm-thick
  slices

1 large yellow capsicum,
  seeded and cut into 1cm-
  thick slices

300ml dry white wine

250g cherry tomatoes, halved

200ml tomato passato (puree)

1 bay leaf

salt and pepper

½ cup parsley, roughly
  chopped

METHOD

 Joint the chicken into eight pieces. Wash them well and pat dry. Heat 3 tablespoons of the olive oil in a pan. Dredge the chicken pieces in the flour and fry in the oil till brown on both sides. Remove and place on some kitchen paper to drain.

 In a fresh pan, heat the rest of the olive oil and fry the onion, garlic, celery heart and capsicum on a high heat, stirring constantly for 4-5 minutes. Add the white wine and cook till all the liquid has evaporated.

 Add the cherry tomatoes, passato and bay leaf. Stir and cook for 5 minutes. Add the chicken pieces and turn down to a simmer. Add a good pinch or two of salt and a couple of turns of pepper. Simmer for 10 minutes then turn the chicken pieces. If the liquid reduces too much add some hot water. Test to see if the chicken is done by piercing near the bone for blood. Once cooked, add the parsley, check for seasoning and remove from the heat. Rest for 5 minutes before serving.

Serves 4

ZUCCHINI

More often than not, when a recipe lists zucchini, small specimens are called for. And for good reason; they're sweeter, crisper and don't contain as much water. This is all well and good but, during their peak season of late spring and summer, larger zucchini are plentiful and inexpensive and if they are growing in the garden, you'll more than likely be left with some the size of small footballs.

Not to worry. After you've stuffed their flowers early in the season with all manner of things including goat's cheese, ricotta, breadcrumbs, herbs and so on, and you've had your fill of small-to-medium zucchini in ratatouille, frittata, braises and the like, the larger ones can be just as useful.

The trick with larger zucchini is first to remove as much water as possible by salting and then thoroughly squeezing the water out. Frying in sweet, extra virgin olive oil concentrates the flavour and results in a crisp texture.

Zucchini go with

Extra virgin olive oil; butter; onions; garlic; tomatoes; eggplant; capsicum; cumin; coriander; chilli; paprika; herbs such as parsley, thyme, basil and oregano; cheese, especially parmesan, gruyere, goat's cheese and pecorino; breadcrumbs; nuts such as almonds, hazelnuts, walnuts and pinenuts; vinegar; anchovies; capers.

Zucchini fritters

INGREDIENTS

500g medium-large zucchini, peeled
4 pinches salt
2 eggs
50g plain flour
50g breadcrumbs
salt and pepper
100ml extra virgin olive oil

METHOD

- Grate the zucchini into a bowl. Sprinkle with a couple of pinches of salt and mix well. Place in a colander to drain for 15 minutes. Squeeze well and place into a bowl. Add the eggs, flour, breadcrumbs, a couple of good pinches of salt and pepper. Mix everything together until it is well amalgamated. Rest in the fridge for an hour.
- Form the mixture into fritters about 5mm thick and fry in olive oil till golden. Drain on kitchen paper before serving with tomato sauce or just a squeeze of lemon.

Serves 4

Grilled and marinated zucchini

INGREDIENTS

400g zucchini, well washed and stem end trimmed
50ml extra virgin olive oil, for brushing
150ml extra virgin olive oil
50ml white wine vinegar
4 garlic cloves, peeled and finely sliced
handful of mint leaves
salt and pepper

METHOD

- Slice the zucchini lengthwise at about 2mm thick. Brush the slices with the olive oil and grill on a flat-grill or barbecue. In a terrine mould or similar ceramic container place a layer of the grilled zucchini slices. Add some of the oil and vinegar mixture, some garlic slices and mint leaves.
- Repeat procedure until all the zucchini have been used, seasoning each layer with salt and pepper. Make sure the top layer of zucchini is covered completely by the oil and vinegar. If not add some more oil to cover.
- Cover with cling film and set in the refrigerator for two days before using. Can be used as part of the antipasto or as an accompaniment to fish and crustaceans.

Serves 4

Fried zucchini with skordalia

INGREDIENTS

Skordalia

2 garlic cloves, peeled

2 pinches salt

70g day-old, white bread, crusts removed and torn into bits

150ml warm milk

freshly ground pepper

1½ tbsp red wine vinegar

100ml extra virgin olive oil

Zucchini

2 large zucchini (80g each), sliced on the diagonal, 5mm thick

salt and pepper

self-raising flour

½ cup extra virgin olive oil

squeeze of lemon juice

METHOD

- This recipe has been adapted from Simon Hopkinson's *Week In Week Out*.
- For the skordalia, put the garlic into a mortar with a couple of pinches of salt and grind to a paste. Soak the bread in the milk for a few minutes until spongy. Squeeze out excess milk and put bread into a food processor with the garlic, a couple of turns of pepper and the vinegar. Pulse and add oil in a thin stream until it is thick and paste-like. Don't overwork; a little texture is desirable.
- Sprinkle zucchini slices with a little salt and drain in a colander for 15 minutes. Pat dry, sprinkle with pepper and dredge in the flour. Fry in olive oil until golden, drain on absorbent paper and serve with skordalia, squeezing lemon juice over them.

Serves 2

BANANAS

In March 2006, Cyclone Larry flattened 80 per cent of Australia's banana crop in North Queensland, mostly in the Innisfail and Tully areas as well as the Atherton Tablelands.

The day after, the Australian Banana Growers Council chief executive, Tony Heidrich, suggested prices would more than likely double. The people's fruit reached more than $10 a kilogram in some parts, more than three times the pre-Larry level.

It took 18 months for the Queensland banana industry to get back to a relatively normal situation but one of the positives during the height of the shortage was the increased availability of fruit from the banana coast of NSW.

For me, the most flavoursome bananas in the country come from the area between Yarrahappini, just south of Macksville, to Woolgoolga, just north of Coffs Harbour. They're smaller, sweeter and tastier because they take longer to grow than their Queensland counterparts.

For breakfast, serve the grilled banana with toasted almonds with porridge or, if rushed, make a quick smoothie with banana, maple syrup, vanilla, nutmeg and a spoonful of LSA (ground linseed, sunflower and almond). The "fingers" can be cut into small bite-sized pieces and served with coffee or tea, or as part of a composed dessert with icecream, custard or sago coconut pudding.

Roast bananas stuffed with apples and amaretti

INGREDIENTS

6 large bananas, not too ripe
4 granny smith apples, peeled, cored and cut into chunks
60g caster sugar
6 tbsp water
2 tbsp grappa or brandy
300ml cream
120g amaretti biscuits, crumbled
50g unsalted butter, melted

METHOD

◉ This recipe has been adapted from Luigi Veronelli's *I Dolci Secondo Veronelli* published by Rizzoli in 1982.

◉ Wash and dry the bananas well and cut them in half, with the skin on, and remove the flesh making sure not to damage the peel. Place the apples and sugar in a saucepan with the water and cook until the pieces are soft. Remove and pass the apples and their liquid through a sieve. Return the sieved apple to the saucepan, add the grappa and 50ml of the cream and boil gently until the mixture has thickened – about 2-3 minutes.

◉ Place the 12 banana peel halves on a baking tray and fill with the apple-cream mixture. Slice the banana flesh halves and place them on top of the apple-cream mixture. Sprinkle the bananas with the crumbled amaretti and a little caster sugar. Spoon the melted butter on top and place in a preheated 200C oven until the tops are golden brown – about 8 minutes or so.

Serves 12

Bananas go with

Sugar; treacle; honey; palm sugar; maple syrup; caramel; coconut; tapioca; sago; rice; yoghurt; cream; milk; coconut cream and milk; icecream and gelato; custard; pastry, especially puff and sweet shortcrust; lemon; lime; apple; pineapple; mango; passionfruit; lychee; vanilla; nutmeg; cinnamon; hazelnut; almond.

Caramelised banana and roast macadamia fingers

Grilled bananas with toasted almonds

Grilled bananas with toasted almonds

INGREDIENTS

2 tbsp unsalted butter, melted

juice of 1 lime

¼ cup strained fresh orange juice

¼ tsp ground nutmeg

¼ tsp ground cardamom

4 firm bananas

¼ cup brown sugar

2 tbsp blanched, sliced almonds

METHOD

🍽 This recipe is adapted from Yumana Devi's *The Art of Indian Vegetarian Cooking.*

🍽 Preheat the grill. Cover a baking tray with non-stick baking paper and brush with melted butter. Combine the lime and orange juice, nutmeg and cardamom in a small dish. Peel the bananas and cut each in half, top to bottom. Place on the baking tray, cut side up. Spoon the juice over the bananas and drizzle with the remaining butter, then with the brown sugar. Grill until the surface bubbles and is lightly brown.

🍽 Remove and sprinkle the almonds on top. Return to the grill until the almonds are toasted. Serve immediately.

Serves 4

Caramelised banana and roast macadamia fingers

INGREDIENTS

2 medium-sized bananas, still firm but not green

100g macadamia, unsalted and roasted

150g caster sugar

1 tsp ground cardamom

125g unsalted butter

4 sheets filo pastry

2 tbsp honey

METHOD

🍽 Peel the bananas and slice them, top to bottom, into eight long pieces. Put the roasted macadamia, caster sugar and cardamom into a mortar or food processor and grind until fine. Melt the butter gently in a saucepan on very low heat. Lay out the filo sheets one at a time and brush the surface facing up with the melted butter. Sprinkle the sheet with the ground macadamia, taking care to leave 3-4cm on each long end free of the nuts. Cut the sheet in half, top to bottom, with a knife.

🍽 Take a piece of banana and put it at the beginning of one of the prepared filo ends. Don't worry if it is curved and it breaks. Roll it up gently but making sure it's as tight as possible. Repeat until you have eight "fingers". Place them on some non-stick baking paper on an oven tray and refrigerate for an hour or freeze until you want to use them.

🍽 To bake, add the honey to the remaining butter and heat gently then mix well. Preheat the oven to 180C. Brush each finger well with the butter-honey mixture and place in the oven.

🍽 After 10 minutes, turn the fingers and baste with the caramelised liquid forming on the tray. Bake for another 10 minutes, remove and cool on a wire rack. Serve with vanilla icecream.

Makes 8 fingers

SUGAR

Sugar cane is generally thought to have originated to our immediate north, in New Guinea. There are hundreds of wild varieties of sugar cane growing there but this bamboo-like grass is now cultivated throughout many of the world's tropical and sub-tropical regions.

Highly refined white sugar is easy to use because it is essentially tasteless, as all the molasses has been removed.

Much of our cooking is based on its inherent properties, not least of which is sweetness. But in recent years there has appeared on supermarket, specialist and health store shelves a variety of cane sugars that merit attention.

As with brown and dark-brown sugar, Australia produces black sugar. All three derive from a similar process of refining the sugar then adding back the molasses. The difference in colour is indicative of the amount of molasses contained – the more molasses, the stronger the flavour and moister the sugar.

More interesting is rapadura sugar. It is made from the dried sugar-cane juice containing all its molasses. In this process the sugar is formed into a dry, hard brick and then ground down to a coarse, light brown powder.

The powder is dry compared to the brown sugars, is not as sweet and has a delicate vanilla-caramel flavour. Try it on porridge, in cakes (especially banana cake) or desserts where colour is not an issue.

Darker in colour and richer in flavour is Colombian piloncillo and Indian jaggery. These sugars are set in the form of a cake. Grate or shave straight onto custard, cereal, icecream or substitute for brown sugar where a rich caramel or molasses flavour is required.

Hot butterscotch with icecream and caramelised pastry

INGREDIENTS

8cm square of puff pastry
3 tbsp caster sugar
400g brown, black or rapadura
    sugar
250ml cream
200g unsalted butter
vanilla icecream

METHOD

- Roll the puff pastry into a rectangle 10-12cm wide. Sprinkle the caster sugar onto the pastry and roll it in with the rolling pin. Cut into 1cm-wide sticks, twisting each three or four times. Rest in the refrigerator on baking trays for 30 minutes. Bake in a preheated 220C oven until the sugar begins to caramelise, then turn the sticks and finish baking them. Cool and store in an airtight container.
- To make the butterscotch, heat the dark sugar, cream and butter in a saucepan, whisking until the butter is entirely incorporated. Scoop some vanilla icecream in serving coupes, spoon some hot butterscotch over it and serve with the caramelised pastry sticks.

Serves 6-8

Pinenut and rosemary praline

INGREDIENTS

360g glucose
360g sugar divided into three
    lots of 120g
100g pinenuts, toasted
2 tbsp rosemary, dried

METHOD

- Dissolve the glucose gently in a pot over a medium flame. Add the first lot of 120g of sugar and mix until melted. Repeat with the next two batches of sugar, one at a time. Keep cooking and mixing until the sugar colour is golden brown. Add the pinenuts and rosemary, mix well and turn out on silicon paper on a tray. Let cool completely. Break into shards and pound or put in food processor till it is fine like coarse sand. Perfect for folding into vanilla gelato, sprinkling on custards or as a topping for cakes. Store in an airtight container in a cool cupboard.

Makes about 750ml of praline

Lemon confit

INGREDIENTS

500g white sugar

500ml water

5-6 medium-sized lemons

METHOD

🍽 Preheat the oven to 150C. Place the sugar and water in a saucepan and bring to the boil. Lower heat and simmer for 2 minutes until all the sugar has dissolved.

🍽 Wash the lemons well and trim about 5mm from both ends of each. Cut the lemons into thin slices and remove any seeds. Lay the lemon slices in a baking pan in rows, each slightly overlapping the next. Add the sugar syrup gently over the lemon slices so they are covered.

🍽 Place a piece of baking paper, randomly pricked all over with a sharp knife to allow moisture to escape, on top of the lemon and cover the baking pan with foil. Bake in the oven for about 50-60 minutes until the lemon slices are translucent. Remove the foil and continue baking for a further 30-40 minutes until the sugar is syrupy. Remove from the oven and cool before using. It will keep refrigerated in its syrup for weeks. Use the lemon slices for custard tarts, decorations for cakes or any citrus dessert.

Serves 8

Sugar goes with

Cream; milk; pastry; tomatoes; carrots; onions; chilli; some curries; porridge; vanilla; cardamom; clove; cinnamon; nutmeg; star anise; pepper; Thai dressings; Chinese red-braised dishes; sweet polenta.

ORANGES

Oranges can be divided into two groups: sweet and bitter. The sweet include the navel and blood oranges and are best eaten fresh – especially the navel, because once squeezed its juice turns sour quickly.

It seems the culprit, present in the navel, is a compound called linonin. The bitter orange group, of which the Seville orange is the most common, doesn't contain this compound so its flavour, though bitter, is pleasant.

If you've ever followed a recipe calling for orange juice and it has turned out to be a bitter disappointment, chances are the problem is the navel orange.

The bitter orange has, however, been part of Mediterranean and Middle Eastern cooking for a very long time, so most of the traditional dishes using oranges are based on the Seville rather than the sweeter navel, which was a later introduction from China.

If you want to make duck a l'orange, Arabic naranjiya (lamb stewed in orange juice), Spanish caldillo de perro ("dog soup"), Israeli oaf tapuzim (chicken with oranges) or any other preparation that relies on orange juice, choose your fruit wisely.

Oranges go with
Cream; mascarpone; yoghurt; olives; onion; fennel; strawberries; mint; pineapple; crab; prawns; fish stew; beef stew; duck; goose; lamb; chicken; pork; chocolate; sugar; honey; beetroot; extra virgin olive oil; red wine vinegar; sponge cake; almonds; kirsch; Cointreau; grand marnier; grappa.

Grilled duck breasts with Seville orange sauce

INGREDIENTS

1 litre duck, chicken or veal stock
3 Seville oranges
2 tsp sugar
3 tbsp red wine vinegar
6 duck breast fillets, skin on
salt and pepper

METHOD

- Make the sauce first by boiling the stock until it reduces to about 200ml.
- Using a vegetable peeler, remove the zest from the oranges in strips, making sure the white bitter pith is not removed as well. Bring a pot of water to the boil and blanch the zest for 3 minutes. Drain and cut the zest pieces into fine julienne (matchsticks).
- Juice the oranges and strain to remove any seeds or pith. Place the sugar and vinegar in a saucepan and bring to the boil. Turn the heat down a little and continue boiling until the mixture is thick and caramelised. Add the orange juice and half the julienned zest and reduce to a thick syrup. Add the 200ml of reduced stock and bring back to the boil. Season with a little salt and pepper. The sauce can be made days ahead of time and reheated when needed.
- To cook the ducks, first preheat the oven to 250C. Salt the skin side on each of the breasts and place them skin-side down in a frypan that can transfer to the oven. Turn the flame to high. This will crisp the skin as well as removing (rendering) most of the fat so that the duck pieces are ready for the oven. Once the skin is firm, remove the rendered fat from the pan and, still skin-side down, place the pan with the duck breasts in the oven for 7-8 minutes.
- Remove, rest for 10 minutes, and serve the duck breasts with the reheated sauce with the addition of the remaining julienned zest.

Serves 6

Navel orange with dark chocolate

Candied and dried orange peel

INGREDIENTS

oranges

sugar

water

METHOD

🍽 For both candied and dried orange peel, start by using a vegetable peeler to peel strips of orange skin, taking care to remove as little as possible of the white pith beneath. To dry the peel, simply thread the strips using a needle and hang them up away from direct sunlight.

🍽 To candy, slice the strips thinly, add enough water to just cover the strips and bring to the boil. Take them from the heat, strain and run them under cold water to refresh. Repeat the process and then, the third time, add a mixture of half sugar, half water to cover the peel and bring to a simmer. Keep simmering till the water reduces and a thick syrup is left. Store the candied peel in the syrup in a jar and place in the refrigerator.

INGREDIENTS

oranges

sugar

brandy, cognac or armagnac

good quality dark chocolate

METHOD

🍽 Allow two navel oranges per person. Slice the skin and pith off to reveal the bright flesh, then cut the individual segments into a bowl with a little sugar and, if you like, 3-4 tablespoons of brandy, cognac or armagnac. Once all the segments are cut, all that remains is the frame of each orange. Take the frame and, with your hands, squeeze the juice into the bowl (the alcohol seems to stop the juice from becoming bitter). Mix it gently to dissolve the sugar, taking care not to damage the segments, and leave for at least an hour.

🍽 Serve the marinated segments in small bowls with some finely chopped, good quality dark chocolate and finish with some candied orange peel on top.

Serves 1

BROAD BEANS

It's a bit of a race with broad beans. Once they start in early spring they're small and delicate, their foetus-like shell every bit as sweet as the bean inside. It's just a matter of prising them from their downy casing and cooking them gently or, as they do in the Mediterranean, eating them raw as a snack with some sharp cheese and a glass of local wine.

But as the temperature starts to rise, the pods get bigger and so do the beans inside. The shell thickens and is too tough and bitter to cook. It has to be double peeled – firstly out of the pod and then prised from the light green shell to reveal the jade seed within. You'll know when the season is about to finish because more often these seeds will be yellow, tough and dry.

In mid-season look for pods that are fresh and green with no black spots or blemishes. Use them anywhere peas are used. Toss them through some just-cooked pasta with pecorino, a little olive oil and some freshly chopped tomato. They are particularly good accompanying crispy skinned duck with balsamic vinegar.

Broad beans go with
Butter; extra virgin olive oil; cream; salty, aged cheeses; pan-fried and roast veal; poached or roast chicken; roast duck; braised pork belly; prosciutto and bacon; cooked prawns; grilled fish; rocket; radicchio; cos; roast tomato; garlic; basil; mint; borage; marjoram; thyme; parsley.

Salad of roasted eggplant, onion, tomato and broad beans

INGREDIENTS

1-2 medium eggplants, cut into eight 1cm-thick slices, all about the same size

2 large sweet onions, cut into eight 1cm-thick slices, as with eggplant

2 large tomatoes, cut into eight 1cm-thick slices, as with eggplant

16 thin shavings of parmesan

200g broad beans, double peeled and blanched in boiling water for 1 minute

2 cups chopped rocket leaves

3 tbsp extra virgin olive oil

2 tbsp red wine vinegar

salt and pepper

METHOD

- Preheat oven to 220C. Sprinkle a little salt on both sides of each slice of eggplant. Wait 10 minutes then pat dry each slice with a towel. Brush each slice of the eggplant and the onion with the olive oil, place on a baking tray and roast until the eggplant is golden brown and the onion is soft but doesn't fall apart – about 10-12 minutes.
- To assemble the dish, stack in sequence: one eggplant slice, one tomato, two parmesan shards and the onion, seasoning as you go. Repeat again, concluding with the onion on top. Toss the broad beans and the chopped rocket with extra virgin olive oil and the vinegar, season and arrange around each stack.

Serves 4

Crusty eggs with broad beans and chives

INGREDIENTS

2 tbsp extra virgin olive oil

½ cup sourdough crumbs, not too fine

4 eggs

½ cup broad beans, double-peeled and blanched 30 seconds in boiling water

2 tbsp finely sliced chives

2 tbsp parmesan, finely grated

salt and pepper

METHOD

- Heat the olive oil in a 22cm frypan on a medium heat. Add the breadcrumbs, making sure that they are evenly distributed in the pan and fry for a minute, constantly mixing. Break the four eggs over the breadcrumbs taking care to keep the yolks intact. Keep cooking until the whites have become solid. Add the broad beans and sprinkle the chives and parmesan over the top.
- Finally, season with salt and pepper and serve divided in two.

Serves 2

Crab and broad bean crostoni

INGREDIENTS

2 cups double-peeled broad beans

6 tbsp extra virgin olive oil

200g cooked blue swimmer, spanner or mud crab meat

¼ cup finely chopped coriander

1 or 2 red chillies, finely chopped

6 tbsp freshly squeezed lemon juice

salt and pepper

2 tbsp extra virgin olive oil, for brushing

4 large slices bread, lightly toasted or grilled

1 large garlic clove, cut in two

METHOD

🍽 Plunge the broad beans into boiling, salted water for 2 minutes until soft. Put three-quarters of the cooked, still warm, beans in a bowl with the olive oil and mash them with a fork until roughly pureed. Add the rest of the beans, crab, coriander, chilli and lemon juice and season with salt and pepper to taste. Mix gently, keeping the pieces of crab whole.

🍽 Brush the bread with 2 tablespoons of olive oil and lightly grill or toast it. Rub the grilled bread with the cut face of the garlic pieces. Spread the broad bean and crab mixture on each of the crostini and serve whole or cut into pieces.

Serves 4

SNAPPER

Fish names can be very confusing. The snapper, for instance, is not really a snapper but a bream and, depending where you live on Australia's coast, it is sometimes referred to as red bream or pink snapper.

True snappers are, in fact, sea perch and can be called red snapper, golden snapper or flame snapper, depending on the variety. The red emperor is a true snapper, found in tropical northern waters along with the majority of its relatives.

What we call snapper is essentially a cold-water fish, found all the way around the south, including Tasmania, and halfway up each side of the continent. It is also prolific in New Zealand waters. It's easy to spot, especially with larger fish, as it has a big bony knob on top of its head, above the eyes. Smaller, plate-sized specimens are pinkish in colour with silver-blue spots on the body.

The smaller fish can be handy for individual servings but, for me, the flavour of larger snapper is superior. When the fillet is more than 1.5cm thick, the texture is at its best.

Snapper can be used in a variety of dishes in many styles of cuisine. This meaty fish will hold its own in a chilli-laden curry or a spicy tagine. Fish sauce, sugar and lime dressings can accompany whole, deep-fried preparations or a salad of pan-fried pieces.

After your snapper is filleted, ask to keep the head as it makes the most delicious soup base.

Snapper goes with

Lemon and lime; butter and extra virgin olive oil; capers; olives; most herbs, especially coriander, parsley, fennel, basil, oregano, rosemary; spices such as cumin, paprika, cayenne pepper, fennel seeds and black pepper; chilli; garlic; fish sauce; soy sauce; vinegar; salad leaves, especially sorrel, rocket, radicchio, watercress and endive.

Snapper curry

INGREDIENTS

8 tbsp extra virgin olive oil
4 garlic cloves, sliced
4 shallots, sliced
½ thumb-sized piece ginger, peeled and sliced thinly
400ml coconut milk
6-8 tbsp curry paste
1 tsp tamarind paste
1 tsp sugar
salt to taste
300g eggplant, cut into bite-sized pieces and par-boiled
2 tomatoes, quartered
10 large green chillies, slit lengthwise
600g snapper, cut into bite-sized pieces

METHOD

This simple curry has been adapted from the collection of Nonya recipes in *Mrs Lee's Cookbook* by Lee Chin Koon.

Heat the oil in a frypan. Add the garlic, shallots and ginger and fry until light brown. Add 3 tablespoons of the coconut milk and the curry paste. Lower the heat, add another 3 tablespoons of coconut milk and continue stirring for 3 minutes. Add the remaining coconut milk, tamarind, sugar and a couple of good pinches of salt. Bring to the boil, add the eggplant, tomatoes, chillies and snapper, and simmer gently for 8-10 minutes. Serve with rice.

Serves 4

Pan-fried snapper fillets with fresh peas

INGREDIENTS

4 tbsp extra virgin olive oil
4 snapper fillets, about 150g each, skin left on
2 shallots, peeled and finely sliced
2 garlic cloves, peeled and finely sliced
2 cups peas, shelled and cooked in boiling salted water till tender
2 tbsp unsalted butter
2 tbsp parsley, finely chopped
salt and pepper

METHOD

Heat 2 tablespoons of the olive oil in a frypan, large enough to hold the four snapper fillets. Sprinkle the skin side of each fillet with salt and fry for a couple of minutes per side. Remove from the pan, transfer to a plate and keep warm.

Add the other 2 tablespoons of olive oil to the pan and lightly fry the shallots and garlic till transparent. Add the cooked peas, season with salt and pepper and keep cooking and stirring for a minute. Turn off the heat and add the butter and parsley.

Place the fillets of snapper on plates and spoon the peas and resulting sauce on top.

Serves 4

Snapper, cabbage and roast macadamia salad

INGREDIENTS

600g snapper fillet, scaled but
  skin left on

¼ savoy cabbage

12 ripe cherry tomatoes,
  washed and quartered

6 tbsp extra virgin olive oil

4 tbsp red wine vinegar

100g macadamia pieces

3 tbsp extra virgin olive oil,
  for frying

salt and pepper

METHOD

🍽 Prepare the snapper fillets by removing any scales left on by
the fishmonger. Cut each fillet down both sides of the central
backbone line, eliminating any bones and leaving two boneless
pieces per fillet. Cut these into large, bite-sized pieces and
refrigerate. Slice the cabbage as thinly as possible and place in a
bowl with the tomatoes, olive oil and vinegar. Season with salt
and pepper and toss. Leave it for at least half an hour, tossing
occasionally.

🍽 Place the macadamia pieces in a dry frypan and place over
medium heat, stirring or tossing, until they are light golden-
brown. Add to the cabbage and toss. Spoon the cabbage onto
serving plates. Heat the olive oil for frying in a large skillet or
on the hotplate of a barbecue. Sprinkle the snapper pieces with
some salt and fry them quickly at high heat until they are just
cooked. Distribute the pieces amongst the plates and serve
immediately.

Serves 4

LAMB SHOULDER

Lamb is easy to find all year round yet spring lamb seems to taste better because there is lush, new grass for them to feed on.

According to the Meat and Livestock Association, spring accounts for 31 per cent of total yearly lamb production and lamb is the last of our red meat that is still grass fed.

The prime cuts such as cutlets, loin and leg are the most popular and easiest to use.

The shoulder, however, is the most versatile. It can cope with a wide range of cooking methods because it contains a little more fat, keeping it moist and succulent when poached, roasted, slow braised or barbecued.

Poaching lamb shoulder is not often done. A 2kg shoulder, with its three bones intact, will fit into a decent-sized pot. Follow the cooking instructions as per the salad recipe. Once cooled a little, the meat can be stripped from the bones and simply dressed with some good olive oil and vinegar.

It sounds basic and it is. Just put a few slices in a bread roll with some butter lettuce and tomato and you've got a great panino (Italian sandwich).

For something more substantial, add the poached meat to some roast vegetables, salad leaves and your signature dressing.

Bollito of spring lamb shoulder with mustard fruit cos and radicchio salad

INGREDIENTS

1 lamb shoulder, about 2.5kg, trimmed of excess fat and skin

2 carrots, peeled and cut into chunks

1 onion, peeled and cut into quarters

1 stick of celery, cut into 2cm lengths

1 leek, cleaned, trimmed and cut into 2cm rounds

large handful of chopped parsley

1 cos heart, sliced thick across the leaves

1 radicchio heart, sliced across the leaves

6 tbsp extra virgin olive oil

4 tbsp balsamic vinegar

salt and pepper

2 tbsp mustard fruits, chopped finely

METHOD

🍽 Place the lamb shoulder into a pot of cold water so that it is well covered. Add the carrots, onion, celery and leek. Bring to the boil, then cover and simmer until the meat is tender – this should take about 80-100 minutes for a 2.5kg shoulder. When it is done, take it off the heat and leave to cool in its broth. Strain the broth and keep in the refrigerator as a soup base.

🍽 Once cool (but not cold) the meat should come off the bone easily and can be sliced.

🍽 Put the parsley, cos and radicchio together with the sliced shoulder in a salad bowl, add the olive oil and toss. Add the balsamic vinegar and season.

🍽 Plate the salad and finish with a little dollop of the chopped mustard fruit on top.

Serves 8

Lamb shoulder goes with

Extra virgin olive oil; butter; herbs such as rosemary, sage, tarragon, oregano and marjoram; tomato; onions; garlic; leeks; zucchini; eggplant; capsicum; potato; parsnips; fennel; celeriac; carrots; red and white wine; vinegar; capers; anchovies; olives; bread; rice.

Roast lamb shoulder with tarragon and bread stuffing

Lamb shoulder, cos and fennel salad

INGREDIENTS

1 onion, finely diced

6 garlic cloves, minced

80g butter

2 cups breadcrumbs

100g parmesan, grated

½ cup tarragon leaves, roughly chopped

salt and pepper

1 lamb shoulder, blade bone removed and butterflied open (your butcher will do this)

2 tbsp extra virgin olive oil

METHOD

Make the stuffing by lightly frying the onion and garlic in the butter until they are soft but not burnt. Cool a little before adding the breadcrumbs, parmesan and tarragon. Season with salt and pepper and mix well.

Open up the lamb shoulder, skin side down on the bench and place the stuffing in the middle, rolling the shoulder like a jam roll. Using butcher's twine, tie the shoulder securely and place in a baking dish. Cover the skin with the olive oil, season with salt and pepper and roast in a preheated 220C oven for 20 minutes. Lower the temperature to 120C and leave for another 20-30 minutes. Remove from the oven, place some foil over the top and rest for 5-10 minutes before slicing and serving.

Serves 4

INGREDIENTS

1 lamb shoulder, about 2.5kg, trimmed of excess fat and skin

2 carrots, cut in chunks

1 onion, peeled and quartered

1 stick of celery, cut into 2cm lengths

1 cos heart, sliced thickly

1 fennel bulb, trimmed, sliced thinly

6 tbsp extra virgin olive oil

4 tbsp red wine vinegar

large handful chopped parsley

1 cup pitted black olives

freshly cracked pepper

sea salt

METHOD

Place the shoulder, bone in, into a pot of cold water so that it is well covered. Add the carrots, onion and celery. Bring to the boil, then simmer until the meat is tender. This should take about 45-60 minutes depending on size. When it is done, take it off the heat and cool in its broth.

Once cool (but not cold) the meat should come off the bone easily and can be sliced in bite-sized pieces. The remaining broth can be kept in the refrigerator as a soup base.

Put the cos and fennel together with the sliced shoulder in a salad bowl, dress with the olive oil and vinegar, add the parsley and olives, season and toss well.

Serves 6-8 as a first course

ARTICHOKES

The artichoke is the edible flower of a type of thistle, which may be the reason why many people are reticent when it comes to its preparation. Some varieties can have nasty thorns at the tips of their leaves but others are small, delicate and positively non-threatening. What is certain is that the artichoke, with its bitter flavour and unique texture, is one of the gems of the Mediterranean.

There are small, green, perfectly round ones the size of a golf ball that can be pared back, sliced thinly and added raw to a salad. Larger ones can be blanched (see recipe) and served whole in the conventional manner, with garlic mayonnaise or extra virgin olive oil for dipping the tender leaf ends.

The purple, thornier artichokes often have the best flavour. The tops can be removed, with their spikes, using a large knife, cutting straight through halfway up the head. The tough outer leaves are now easy to pull away. Depending on their size, they can be halved or quartered and stewed with white wine, vinegar, garlic, leeks and parsley until tender.

Look for artichokes that are youthful. If left too long on the plant, the heart will flower and become woody. Artichokes should be fully closed, waxy and bright, no matter the colour.

Artichokes go with
Extra virgin olive oil; butter; cheese, especially parmesan, gruyere, pecorino and goat's milk; vinegar; lemon; roast capsicum; onion; garlic; zucchini; asparagus; potato; tomato; mint; coriander; parsley; oregano; marjoram; all salad leaves; veal; beef; tuna; swordfish; prawns.

Basic blanched artichokes

INGREDIENTS

juice of 1 lemon
2 bay leaves
10 whole peppercorns
2 good pinches of salt
8 fresh artichokes

METHOD

🍳 Fill a large pot to three-quarters with cold water and add the lemon juice, bay leaves, peppercorns and salt.

🍳 With a sharp paring knife take the top of each artichoke clean off a third of the way from the top, then peel off the dark outer leaves until you reach the tender light green ones. Leave 3-5cm of stalk at the base. Put each artichoke, as it is prepared, in the pot with the acidulated water. The artichokes float, so place a plate on top to keep them submerged.

🍳 Place the pot on the stove and bring to the boil. Turn down to a simmer for a few minutes. To see if they are cooked pierce one in the heart with a sharp knife. If it has little resistance it is cooked. Remove the artichokes with tongs and place upside down on a tray to drain. Trim back the outer leaves and some stalk if necessary. The artichokes are now ready for salads, stuffing and baking, frying or just chopping through pasta.

Serves 4

Artichokes with egg, capers and spring herbs

INGREDIENTS

1 onion, finely chopped

25g capers, well washed

1 cup finely chopped spring herbs (parsley, tarragon, chives and chervil)

3 tbsp white wine vinegar

1 cup extra virgin olive oil

salt and pepper

4 large or 8 small artichokes, blanched (see previous recipe)

4 eggs, hard boiled

4 tbsp chives, finely sliced

METHOD

🍽 Soak the chopped onion in water for 5 minutes, rinse and place in a food processor with the capers, chopped herbs and vinegar. Turn it on and slowly add the olive oil in a fine stream to produce a mayonnaise-like sauce. Finish by adding salt and pepper to taste. Place in a container and store in the refrigerator until needed.

🍽 Open the heads of the blanched artichokes by pulling their leaves back and cut their bases so they sit upright. Arrange on serving plates with slices of the hard-boiled eggs. Drizzle the sauce over and finish with a sprinkling of chopped chives.

Serves 4 as a first course

Artichoke risotto

INGREDIENTS

1 medium onion, finely diced

100g unsalted butter

300g carnaroli rice

1 cup dry white wine

3 litres chicken stock

4 large artichokes, cooked and each cut into eight pieces

olive oil

½ cup grated parmesan cheese

salt and pepper

METHOD

🍽 Sauté the onion in the oil and half of the butter. Before it is browned, add the rice and stir at medium heat till it is transparent – 2 minutes.

🍽 Add the wine and let it boil away. In a separate pot, heat the stock. Add three ladles of the hot stock and stir. Keep cooking the risotto, gradually adding hot stock as needed. When it is almost ready add the artichokes, the rest of the butter and two good handfuls of grated parmesan. Stir, turn off the heat and cover.

🍽 Let it rest for 2-3 minutes, then add salt and pepper to taste. Serve with more grated parmesan cheese.

Serves 6

SUMMER

WHITE PEACHES

It's often said that we eat with our eyes, but it could be equally true that we taste with our noses. This is especially evident during summer when a ripening fruit seems to summon us with its scent.

Walk into any good fruit shop and take a long whiff. Perhaps the most dominant aroma, above even that of mango, is peach.

White peaches have an especially beautiful scent, with a bouquet that is delicate, yet piercing.

The peach is a member of the rose family, and its fragrance, particularly that of the white peach, is reminiscent of its famous perfumed relative.

To really enjoy the flavour of a white peach there is no better way than to eat one raw, in the peak of condition, but it's also the essential ingredient in a bellini, the famous Italian aperitif made from five parts prosecco (an Italian sparkling wine) and one part white peach puree.

Invented in 1948 at Harry's Bar in Venice by head barman Giuseppe Cipriani, the bellini is a perfect summer drink, made more special by the relatively short white peach season.

White peaches are available from early December to early March. White nectarines are in season about a month earlier and can be substituted in recipes that call for white peaches.

What to look for: sweetness, perfume, flavour and lusciousness. A good way to tell if a peach is going to have good flavour is to smell it. If the perfume is strong and sweet, then chances are the taste will follow.

Peaches stuffed with amaretti and chocolate

INGREDIENTS
4 large, ripe yellow peaches
2 eggs
40g caster sugar
30g good quality, unsweetened cocoa powder
100g amaretti biscuits, crumbled
4 tsp unsalted butter

METHOD
- Bring a pot of water to the boil and immerse the peaches, holding them under, for 30 seconds. Plunge them into ice water. Once cool, remove their skin and cut each in half. Remove the seed and, with a teaspoon, make the cavity in each peach half twice its original size.
- In a bowl, whisk the eggs and sugar together. Whisk in the cocoa powder. Add the crumbled amaretti biscuits.
- Fill each peach halves' cavity with the mixture and arrange in an oven dish. Place half a teaspoon of butter on top of each peach half and bake in a preheated 170C oven for 20-25 minutes.
- Remove and cool to room temperature before serving.

Serves 4

White peaches go with
Dessert wines, especially moscato d'Asti and late-picked semillon; sparkling wines, especially prosecco; orange/lemon peel; almond, pistachio and hazelnut; amaretto; rosewater; stone fruit; gelato and icecream; vanilla; cardamom, cinnamon and cassia bark; mint; camomile; cream; mascarpone; custard; sugar, especially brown and demerara; cognac and armagnac.

Roasted white peaches with camomile, vanilla and prosecco

Brandied white peaches on toast

INGREDIENTS

4 medium-sized white peaches
orange rind
brandy
brown sugar
slices of brioche, panettone or fruit bread
cream

METHOD

🍽 Peel fresh white peaches and cut into slices. Place them in a bowl, then finely grate the rind of one orange over them. Drizzle on a generous quantity of brandy (cognac or armagnac is best).

🍽 Finally, sprinkle on a little brown sugar and let them macerate for at least an hour. To serve, toast slices of brioche, panettone or fruit bread. Smother generously with thick cream and place the peach slices on top, drizzled with the brandy juices.

Serves 4

INGREDIENTS

8-12 white peaches
1 bottle of prosecco
1 cup sugar
2 cardamom pods
1 vanilla bean (split)
¼ cup camomile flowers

METHOD

🍽 Allow 2-3 peaches per person depending on the size of the fruit. Cut the peaches in half and remove the stone. Arrange in an ovenproof dish. Into a saucepan, pour a bottle of prosecco. Add a cup of sugar, two cardamom pods, a vanilla bean (split) and camomile flowers. Bring to boil, then turn down the heat and simmer for 5 minutes. Strain, pouring over the peaches.

🍽 Place in a preheated 190C oven and roast for 10 minutes. Baste then turn the peaches and roast for another 10 minutes until tender. Cool a little before serving with fresh cream or zabaglione.

Serves 4

SCHOOL PRAWNS

It's January – the middle of summer – and all up and down the east coast of Australia many of us are at our favourite beachside spot relaxing.

For caravan parks, this is the peak season. Everything is booked out, including the noisy high-traffic plots around the amenities block. Even all the mosquito-infested tent sites among the paperbarks down by the river are taken.

Mornings are filled with surfing and swimming, followed by the ever-present smell of bacon and burning toast for breakfast. Days are spent under the shade of the new best friend's annexe, watching the cricket and drinking beer. On balmy evenings, during the dark phases of the moon, the lights of prawning parties dot the inky surface of rivers, estuaries and inlets like fireflies.

From Tin Can Bay in Queensland down to Corner Inlet in Victoria, using hand-drawn drag or scoop nets, they hunt the sweet, firm and moist-fleshed school prawn.

On a good night, the 10-litre bag limit is easily reached. All that's left to do is cook them properly.

It's always best to use seawater but well-salted tap-water will do. Bring it to a rolling boil then drop in the prawns. Remove them after 3-4 minutes, depending on their size, and drain them.

School prawns are one of summer's most memorable pleasures.

Spaghettini with school prawns, anchovies and olives

INGREDIENTS
500g spaghettini
4 tbsp extra virgin olive oil
10 anchovy fillets
15 pitted green olives
500g school prawns, cooked and peeled
handful flat-leaf parsley

METHOD
◉ Boil 500g of spaghettini (thin spaghetti) until it is al dente or firm to the bite. To do this, cook it a minute or two less than it says on the pack. Drain the spaghettini well, transfer it to a large bowl and dress it with extra virgin olive oil. Set it aside to cool.

◉ Meanwhile, chop anchovy fillets and pitted green olives into small pieces and mix them, along with cooked and peeled school prawns, into the cooling spaghettini. Finely chop a handful of flat-leaf parsley leaves and toss into the mix. Check for seasoning and serve.

Serves 4-6

What to look for
Live river prawns are almost translucent, with distinct blue tips and a slippery feel to their shell. During the season, school prawns are available – mostly cooked – at fish markets and co-operatives. Look for bright, firm shells and eyes, with feelers and legs intact, and no discolouration.

School prawns go with
Mayonnaise; extra virgin olive oil; XO sauce; fish sauce; soy sauce; yellow bean sauce; Worcestershire sauce; mirin; oregano; basil; parsley; coriander; chives; cumin; ginger; tamarind; onions; spring onions; shallots; garlic; tomato; coconut; chilli; paprika; cayenne pepper; lemons; limes; eggs.

School prawn, thyme and rocket frittata

School prawns with lettuce Perugian-style

INGREDIENTS

1 garlic clove, minced

¼ cup flat-leaf parsley, chopped fine

100g mixed, Italian-style, pickled vegetables, drained well and chopped finely

1 tsp capers, well washed and dried, chopped fine

juice of 1 lemon

2 tbsp white wine vinegar

150 ml extra virgin olive oil

2 pinches salt

1 small cos lettuce

500g school prawns (or other small prawns), cooked and peeled

METHOD

◎ Place the garlic, parsley, vegetables, capers, lemon juice, vinegar and olive oil in a bowl with a couple of good pinches of salt and whisk energetically until everything is well incorporated.

◎ Wash the lettuce and dry it well. Cut it in fine strips and lay on one large plate or single serving plates.

◎ Sit the peeled prawns on top. Drizzle the dressing over and serve.

Serves 4

INGREDIENTS

2 tbsp extra virgin olive oil

2 eggs

salt and pepper

12 school prawns, cooked and peeled

2-3 sprigs thyme, chopped

rocket leaves, roughly sliced

METHOD

◎ This is a quick, single-serve frittata and can be made almost as quickly as a pancake.

◎ Heat extra virgin olive oil in a skillet until it is just smoking. Beat eggs lightly, season with salt and pepper and pour into the pan. The frittata should spread over the pan quite thinly and only take a minute to cook. Remove from heat and distribute cooked and peeled school prawns onto the egg. Sprinkle chopped sprigs of thyme on top. Transfer to a plate – it should slide easily out of the pan with the help of a fish slice – and finish with roughly sliced rocket leaves.

Serves 2

CHILLI

The warmer the weather, the greater my attraction to fiery foods. In summer, I crave mouth-tingling chilli wontons, palate-numbing green papaya salad and blistering chilli and garlic spaghetti. Craving is perhaps the right word here because the more chilli-hot the food we eat, the more endorphins the body releases and the better it makes us feel.

Chillies are dispersed throughout the world, but it seems the further a country is from the equator, the subtler their use.

Originally from tropical South America, chillies were part of what Alfred Crosby calls "The Columbian Exchange" that occurred progressively after 1492. In his book of the same name, Crosby asks: "What would Mediterranean dishes be like without chiles [sic], or the eastern European diet without paprika, that condiment derived from the chile pepper?" To these cuisines, we can add those of China, India and the subcontinent, Indonesia and all the countries of Asia and Africa.

Chilli goes with
Oil, especially coconut, sesame, peanut and olive; soy sauce; tofu; green vegetables such as spinach, bok choy, silver beet, beans, broccoli, soy beans and choy sum; most fish, especially bream, snapper, flathead and tropical reef varieties; crab; pipis; mussels; clams; lobster; goat's cheese; fresh mozzarella, especially buffalo.

Curried spinach and eggplant

INGREDIENTS
- 6 tbsp peanut oil
- 1 medium-sized eggplant, cut into 2cm cubes
- ½ tsp garam masala
- ½ tsp turmeric
- 3 or more chillies (green, red or dried)
- 1 tsp fennel seed
- 1 tsp coriander seed
- 1 tsp cumin seed
- 1 small cassia quill
- 500g spinach leaves, chopped
- 1 tsp maple syrup
- 2 pinches salt
- juice of 1 lime

METHOD
- This recipe has been adapted from Yamuna Devi's *The Art of Indian Vegetarian Cooking*.
- Heat 4 tablespoons of the peanut oil in a wok or frypan over moderate heat. Fry eggplant until well browned. Drain on paper towels then toss in a bowl with garam masala and turmeric.
- Add remaining 2 tablespoons of peanut oil to a clean wok and heat to just below smoking point. Add three or more whole green, red or dried chillies, fennel seed, coriander seed and cumin seed, and a small cassia quill. Mix then add chopped spinach leaves, maple syrup and a couple of good pinches of salt. Keep cooking and stirring for 3-4 minutes until the spinach has wilted.
- Take from the heat, add the eggplant and stir in the juice of one lime. Serve with rice or flatbread and more lime wedges.

Serves 4

Chilli bean relish with garlic bruschetta

INGREDIENTS

2 tbsp extra virgin olive oil

1 onion, diced

2 garlic cloves, minced

1 tsp minced ginger

1 bay leaf

1 sprig of thyme

½ celery heart, chopped

4-6 hot chillies, sliced

¼ cup white wine vinegar

1 tsp sugar

2 ripe tomatoes, chopped

400g cooked cannellini beans

salt and pepper

METHOD

Heat extra virgin olive oil in a saucepan and add onion, minced garlic cloves and ginger. Lightly fry for 30 seconds then add bay leaf, sprig of thyme, celery heart and hot chillies. Keep frying gently for 2 minutes then add white wine vinegar, sugar, tomatoes and cooked cannellini beans. Simmer for 15-20 minutes until the tomatoes break down.

Add salt and pepper to taste and refrigerate overnight before use. Serve with grilled garlic bruschetta.

Makes about 750ml relish

Roman-style chilli cabbage

INGREDIENTS

12 red banana chillies

½ small cabbage, finely sliced

1 egg

60g parmesan, grated

1 tbsp thyme

½ cup bread, white part only, chopped in small dice

1 onion, peeled and finely minced

2 garlic cloves, finely minced

2 tbsp extra virgin olive oil

salt and pepper

200ml tomato passato (puree)

1 cup breadcrumbs

METHOD

Slit the banana chillies carefully only on one side. Remove the stem end and all the seeds and pith inside, making sure each chilli remains in one piece. Plunge the sliced cabbage into boiling, salted water for 4-5 minutes till tender. Drain and let cool.

Roughly chop the cooked cabbage and place in a bowl. Beat the egg with the parmesan and thyme and add to the cabbage along with the bread, onion, garlic and olive oil. Season with salt and pepper and mix well.

Stuff the chillies with the mixture and lay in a baking dish, stuffing side up. Add a tablespoon of passato to the top of each and sprinkle with breadcrumbs. Add enough water to the baking dish to make a 1cm-deep bath. Place in a preheated 180C for 20 minutes.

Serve at room temperature.

Serves 4-6

CUTTLEFISH

In Australia, cuttlefish have mostly been used as bait or for aquaculture feed. Sure, you'll see them occasionally on restaurant menus and at the fish market, but this cephalopod is seen mostly as a poor cousin to its more famous relative, the squid or calamari.

Cuttlefish flesh is thicker than calamari, and coarser-grained, so it can take a little more cooking and is ideal braised, in soup or a curry. It seems to work well with robust flavours so there's no need to worry about overpowering it.

Cuttlefish contain an ink sac and the ink contained within was used in early photography to attain the distinctive sepia tone. This ink is also a delicacy used to colour and flavour all manner of dishes from risotto to pasta.

In Venice, cuttlefish are cleaned and sliced and fried gently in a pot with chopped onion and parsley. Chopped, ripe tomato is then added as well as a teaspoon of cuttlefish ink. It is then simmered slowly for an hour or so, seasoned with salt and pepper and served with polenta.

Cuttlefish goes with
Extra virgin olive oil; butter; garlic; onions; chilli; soy and XO sauce; balsamic vinegar; fish sauce; ginger; shallots; spring onions; lime; lemon; tomato; eggplant; zucchini; cucumber; asparagus; beans; fennel; olives; capers; parsley; basil; coriander; most lettuces and leaves, especially rocket, watercress and radicchio; mayonnaise.

Cuttlefish cooked in a casserole

INGREDIENTS
- 800g cuttlefish, cleaned
- 2 medium red onions
- 2 garlic cloves
- 1 red capsicum
- 3 tbsp extra virgin olive oil
- 500ml dry white wine
- 500ml water
- salt and pepper
- ½ cup chopped parsley

METHOD
- This is a recipe adapted from Trattoria Parido in the town of Rossano Scalo, Calabria, Italy.
- Cut cuttlefish into 1cm-thick strips. Finely chop red onions, garlic cloves and red capsicum and lightly fry in a casserole dish with the extra virgin olive oil. Turn up the heat, add the cuttlefish as well as the dry white wine and stir until evaporated. Now add the water, bring to the boil, turn down to a very low simmer and cover for 5 minutes. Lift the lid, turn up the heat and boil for 2-3 minutes.
- Season with salt and pepper, add chopped parsley and serve.

Serves 6

Cuttlefish with peas

INGREDIENTS
- 2 tbsp extra virgin olive oil
- 1 small onion, peeled and finely chopped
- 2 garlic cloves, peeled and crushed
- 1 chilli, sliced in half
- 250g cleaned cuttlefish, sliced into 5mm strips
- 250ml dry white wine
- 250g ripe Roma tomatoes, washed well and roughly chopped
- 200g fresh peas, shelled
- 2 good pinches salt, plus extra
- ½ cup parsley, roughly chopped

METHOD
- Heat the olive oil in a pan and lightly fry the onion, garlic and chilli till just coloured. Remove from the pan leaving the oil only. Return the pan to the heat and fry the cuttlefish strips on high heat, constantly moving it around for 3 minutes.
- Add the wine and let it evaporate totally. At this point add the tomatoes and peas and add a couple of good pinches of salt. Simmer gently for 40 minutes, adding a little hot water if it gets too dry.
- Once cooked, add the parsley and add a little salt if needed.

Serves 4

Grilled cuttlefish and eggplant with salsa piccante

INGREDIENTS

500g ripe tomatoes

juice of ½ lemon

1 chilli, chopped

1 garlic clove, minced

good handful chopped basil
leaves

¼ cup extra virgin olive oil

1 medium-sized eggplant

4 tbsp extra virgin olive oil,
for frying

salt

250g cuttlefish, cleaned

METHOD

◉ Peel and seed tomatoes and chop them roughly into 1cm pieces.
Place in a bowl, and add the lemon juice, chopped chilli, minced
garlic clove and chopped basil leaves. Season, add extra virgin
olive oil, stir well and allow to sit for 1 hour.

◉ Meanwhile cut up the medium-sized eggplant into 2cm cubes.
Heat 2 tablespoons of the extra virgin olive oil on a grill or
frypan and fry the eggplant cubes until they have browned and
softened. Season with salt and allow to cool.

◉ Cut cleaned cuttlefish into 4cm-square tiles. Heat 2 tablespoons
of extra virgin olive oil on a skillet and fry the cuttlefish tiles on
high heat until they become golden. Serve on the salsa with the
eggplant scattered over.

Serves 4

GARLIC

Garlic is in season in summer and small bunches of four or so bulbs tied together at their stems are on fruiterer's shelves for all too brief a time. Fresh garlic is different from the dried. First, fresh garlic is always locally grown while most of what is consumed dried is imported and to my mind not very good. Second, the cloves are opaque rather than white and are laden with juice. There's a difference in taste as well. Fresh garlic has a zestier, almost citrus-like flavour.

If you want to reduce the after-effects of garlic, a good trick is to take each clove, unpeeled, and pass it gently over a flame until it "pops". A small jet of flame may burst from the clove. This is a mixture of the volatile oils responsible for the flavour as well as the after-taste escaping. The pungent odour is a sulphur compound called allicin that is made when two volatile oils, contained in the cloves, are mixed as garlic is crushed or cut.

Needless to say, I prefer my garlic potent and active!

Garlic goes with
Most herbs, especially basil, coriander, parsley, sorrel, rosemary and thyme; butter; sesame oil; extra virgin olive oil; soy sauce; lamb; pork; beef; poultry; veal; fish, shellfish and crustaceans; game; tofu; pinenuts; almonds; bread; spinach; beans; zucchini; tomatoes; eggplant; goat's cheese; fresh mozzarella; pasta and rice; lettuce.

Fresh garlic and celeriac soup

INGREDIENTS

2 large celeriac bulbs
6-10 bulbs of fresh garlic or 1 large bulb of dried garlic
chicken stock or water
pinch salt
2 good-sized knobs of butter

METHOD

- Peel celeriac bulbs. Cut the flesh into chunks and place in a saucepan. Peel bulbs of fresh garlic (or large bulb of dried garlic) and add to the celeriac. Cover with either clear chicken stock or water. Season with a good pinch of salt and bring to the boil. Turn down to a simmer and cover with a lid. Simmer until the vegetables are soft. Puree, adding knobs of butter.
- Season and serve hot with grilled bread.

Serves 4

Rigatoni with garlic and three cheeses

INGREDIENTS

2 tbsp extra virgin olive oil
10 garlic cloves, minced
½ cup parsley, roughly chopped
1 litre tomato passato (puree)
2 pinches salt and cracked pepper
600g rigatoni pasta
1 small slice each of fontina and gorgonzola
2 tbsp parmesan, grated
½ cup breadcrumbs

METHOD

- Gently heat the olive oil in a pan and fry the garlic. Once its perfume is evident, add the parsley and stir for a moment. Add a small ladle of hot water and simmer for 2 minutes. Add the passato, a couple of good pinches of salt and a little cracked pepper and simmer for 10 minutes. Cook the pasta according to the instructions on the pack.
- Meanwhile, in a small saucepan, gently heat the three cheeses with 1 or 2 tablespoons of water. Add the melted cheeses to the sauce and mix.
- When the pasta is ready, drain and mix thoroughly with the sauce. Place in a serving bowl and sprinkle the breadcrumbs on top.

Serves 6

Beans with roast garlic and pancetta

INGREDIENTS

2 or more bulbs fresh garlic

50g pancetta (or bacon)

1 tsp extra virgin olive oil

250g greeen beans, trimmed

2 tbsp extra virgin olive oil, for dressing

salt and pepper

METHOD

First of all, roast the garlic in a preheated 170C oven for about 20-30 minutes until soft. Cool a little before peeling the cloves and roughly chopping them into large pieces. Cut pancetta (or bacon) into thin pieces and lightly fry in extra virgin olive oil until crisp. Remove the pancetta from the frying pan and drain on some kitchen paper.

Blanch trimmed green beans until tender, drain and dress with the roast garlic pieces and extra virgin olive oil. Season with salt and pepper, toss and serve with the fried pancetta on top.

Serves 4

GOAT'S CHEESE

There's a particular flavour in goat's milk that seems to be magnified when it is made into cheese. In Australia, we're not really used to cheese with loads of flavour, let alone the sorts of wild, almost gamey flavours you find in a mature goat's cheese.

Don't get me wrong; I don't mind the occasional cheese on toast in front of the telly, but for a long time that was all Australia produced – cheese-on-toast cheese.

The labours of the past 20 years or so of artisan-farmhouse cheesemaking in Australia have produced extraordinary cheeses. Among them are gems made from goat's milk. In particular, look for HOLY GOAT, Woodside, Hobbit Farm, Gympie, Kytren, Milawa, Willowbrae and Jannei goat's cheeses.

Goat's cheese goes with
Bread; extra virgin olive oil; walnut oil; hazelnut oil; vinegars; quince paste; raisins; olives; anchovies; capers; nuts; salad leaves, especially the tastier ones such as radicchio and curly endive; paprika, cumin; pepper, chilli and most herbs.

Goat's cheese with roast beetroot, walnuts and radicchio

INGREDIENTS

16 baby beetroot, each golf-ball size
extra virgin olive oil
salt and pepper
½ cup shelled wlanuts
1 tbsp red wine vinegar
1-2 heads radicchio
4-6 tbsp fresh goat's cheese
6-8 chive spears
2 sprigs flat-leaf parsley

METHOD

- Wash baby beetroot and place them in a roasting pan, toss in a little extra virgin olive oil and season with salt and pepper. Roast in a preheated 180C oven for 30 to 35 minutes, until a knife pierces each easily. Put aside and cool. Spread walnuts on a roasting tray or pan and place in the same oven as the beets. Roast them for about 10 minutes. Put aside and cool.
- Cut the beets in half (leave the skin on if you like – it's delicious) and dress with a little olive oil and red wine vinegar.
- Thinly slice radicchio and dress well with vinaigrette. Place the radicchio on a serving plate as a bed and scatter the roasted beets and walnuts on top. Scatter fresh goat's cheese.
- Finely chop chive spears and flat-leaf parsley and sprinkle over the lot.

Serves 4

Roast tomato and goat's cheese with thyme

Goat's cheese, potato and mushroom terrine

INGREDIENTS

5 large potatoes, peeled and thinly sliced

100g mushrooms, thinly sliced

200g goat's cheese

1 cup parsley, roughly chopped

50g butter

4 tbsp extra virgin olive oil

salt and pepper

METHOD

- Butter a terrine mould and begin with a layer of the potato slices, then a layer of mushroom slices, then some crumbled or sliced goat's cheese. Sprinkle on some parsley, salt and pepper. Repeat this sequence until the terrine mould is full, finishing with a layer of cheese on top.
- Season with salt and pepper and scatter the olive oil and parmesan to finish. Bake in a preheated 190C oven for 30 minutes.
- Scoop out to serve at room temperature with a salad.

Serves 4-6

INGREDIENTS

2 medium-large ripe tomatoes

extra virgin olive oil

salt and pepper

4 slices goat's cheese

1 tsp finely chopped thyme

METHOD

- Cut each tomato in half and place them, cut side up, on a baking tray. Sprinkle the open faces with extra virgin olive oil, salt and pepper.
- Cut the goat's cheese. For this dish I prefer a mature, slightly firmer style, such as a Bouche Blanch from France or a Kervella Rondolet from Western Australia. Place on the tomato faces, sprinkle with more olive oil and scatter finely chopped thyme over the lot. Place in a preheated 170C oven for 12 to 15 minutes until the cheese has melted a little.
- Serve hot or, better still, cooled to room temperature, accompanied by a radicchio or curly endive salad.

Serves 4

GRAPES

There's a certain quality to the light filtered through a canopy of grapevines. We learned that long ago, perhaps when ancient people of the Fertile Crescent settled down in communities and started cultivating grapes to make wine.

A few years ago, terracotta shards with traces of wine residue were found in Iran's Zagros Mountains and dated at more than 7000 years old, well into the Neolithic period.

Certainly the Greeks and Romans favoured eating under the shade of a grapevine, as many people do today.

Growing up in suburban Sydney, my family always had a vine trained high on a substantial frame. It was tended for the delicious autumn fruit as well as the cool, dappled shadow it cast during hot summer days.

European cuisines have their rudimentary beginnings in Neolithic times and the grape and all its products are essential in their dishes. To dress a salad, we need vinegar. To braise beef, marinate game or deglaze a sauce, we need wine. Vine leaves make a perfect pouch for stuffing. Pears are poached in red wine, while peaches are poached in white. Baked apples are best stuffed with macerated muscatels and sultanas.

Grapes go with
Cream, especially when whipped; mascarpone and clotted cream; yoghurt; nuts, especially hazelnuts, walnuts and almonds; sugar, especially brown, rock and demerara; aniseed; cinnamon; star anise; clove; nutmeg; rich meats such as oxtail, pork and terrines; game meats such as venison, quail, pigeon and guineafowl; puff pastry; sponge cake; most cheeses.

Grape and macadamia tart

INGREDIENTS

Sweet tart pastry
350g plain flour
70g caster sugar
pinch salt
½ tsp baking powder
grated zest of 1 lemon
170g unsalted butter, cut into 1cm cubes and kept cold
1 egg (about 65g)
1 egg yolk
60ml double cream

Filling
3 eggs, separated
80g caster sugar
grated zest of 1 orange
1 tbsp grappa (or brandy)
pinch salt
½ tsp vanilla essence
150g macadamia, roasted
500g red grapes

METHOD

- For the pastry, place the flour, sugar, salt, baking powder and lemon zest in a food processor. Pulse so the ingredients are combined well. Add the cold butter cubes and pulse repeatedly until the mixture is like sand.

- In a separate bowl whisk together the egg, yolk and cream. Add this mixture to the food processor ingredients and pulse until the mixture forms a ball. Remove from the processor and flatten the dough out to a disc.

- Refrigerate for 3-4 hours. Once set, roll the pastry out to fit a 24cm-tart tin and rest in the refrigerator while preparing the filling. The pastry does not have to be baked first (blind baked).

- For the filling, use the paddle attachment of an electric mixer to beat the egg yolks, 40g of sugar, zest, grappa and salt together till pale. Beat in the vanilla extract.

- Place the macadamia in a food processor with 20g of the sugar and finely grind.

- Fold the sugar-nut mixture into the egg yolk mixture. Whisk the egg whites, slowly adding the remaining 20g of sugar, until they form soft peaks. Fold the whipped egg whites into the nut mixture.

- Fill the tart shell with the resulting mixture, spreading it evenly. Press the grapes into the soft mixture, distributing them evenly throughout the tart. Bake in a preheated 160C oven for 35-40 minutes.

- Remove from the oven and cool completely before serving.

Serves 10

Muscatel and aniseed schiacciata

Grape jelly

INGREDIENTS

2 litres fresh grape juice

500g sugar

METHOD

- Use either white or black grapes with good flavour. De-stem, wash and juice enough grapes to give 2 litres of liquid. Place in a saucepan and add sugar. Bring to the boil and keep simmering until the liquid is reduced by a third. Skim off any scum on the surface. Once reduced, take from heat and cool a little. Ladle into sterilised jars, seal and store in a cool, dry place.
- Serve black grape jelly with blue and aged cheeses. White grape jelly is ideal for desserts.

Serves 4

INGREDIENTS

3 cups plain flour

2 packets powdered yeast

20g aniseed

100g demerara or coffee sugar

200g muscatels

METHOD

- To make a 20-25cm round or rectangular schiacciata (like a pizza), combine plain flour, powdered yeast and enough warm water to make a soft, easily worked dough. Knead until smooth and place in a bowl covered with cling film to prove for 1 hour. Divide in half and roll out two circles or rectangles, 5mm thick, to fit a pizza or baking tray.
- Place aniseed and demerara or coffee sugar in a mortar and crush until fine. Wash muscatels and roll them in the sugar so that they are coated. Lay half the muscatels on the first sheet of dough and sprinkle half the sugar over.
- Now lay the other sheet of dough on top. Scatter the remaining muscatels, sugar and aniseed on top, pressing them into the dough. Bake in a preheated oven at 250C for 15 minutes. Allow to cool then serve.

Serves 4

ICEBERG LETTUCE

It wasn't such a long time ago that a lettuce meant just one thing: the soccer ball-shaped iceberg. With the introduction of prettier, tastier varieties such as mignonette, butter, cos and radicchio, iceberg was relegated to the status of the unfashionable, with fondues, prawn cocktails, glace cherries and Hawaiian pork.

At the height of the Roman Empire its citizens had access to more than 500 types of edible leaves. They ranged from many types of lettuce, such as those of the *Lactuca sativa* family that form rosette-like heads, to the weedy leaves such as sorrel, rocket and lamb's tongue.

Today Australians can probably find about 30 different salad greens in shops and markets. Even so, iceberg's unique qualities have seen it make a welcome return to respectable society.

It should be appreciated for what it is – a utilitarian-leafed, flavour-absorbing ball with a crisp, refreshing texture.

Iceberg lettuce goes with
Extra virgin olive oil; butter; vinegars; mustard; mayonnaise; bacon; pancetta; prosciutto; sausages; veal; grilled or poached chicken; grilled beef and lamb; parsley; mint; tarragon; coriander; shallots; onion; garlic; carrot; peas; roast pumpkin; roast nuts, especially macadamia, hazelnut and almonds.

Iceberg lettuce with peas

INGREDIENTS

2 tbsp extra virgin olive oil
1 tbsp butter
1 onion, finely sliced
2 garlic cloves, minced
1 small head iceberg lettuce, washed
750g peas, fresh or frozen
salt and pepper
mint or parsley, chopped

METHOD

- Heat extra virgin olive oil and butter in a heavy-bottomed soup pot. Add onion and cloves of garlic. Lightly fry, stirring constantly, for 3 minutes until the onions have softened.
- Chop iceberg lettuce into 2cm-wide strips. Add it to the pot, with fresh or frozen peas. Turn up the heat and stir-fry until the lettuce has wilted. Add enough boiling water so the lettuce and peas are half covered. Cover the pot, turn down the heat and simmer for 20 minutes until the peas are cooked. Season with salt and pepper and add some chopped mint and parsley.
- Serve as a first course with croutons and grated pecorino.

Serves 6

Iceberg lettuce stuffed with veal

INGREDIENTS

6 outer leaves iceberg lettuce

1 tbsp extra virgin olive oil

200g veal mince

1 carrot, finely diced

1 onion, finely diced

1 tbsp chopped rosemary

3 tbsp pinenuts

1 tbsp marjoram leaves

2 garlic cloves, minced

1 egg yolk

salt and pepper

METHOD

◉ Blanch iceberg lettuce leaves quickly in salted, simmering water so they wilt slightly. Lay them on a clean towel to cool and dry.

◉ Heat extra virgin olive oil in a pan and lightly fry veal mince with carrot, onion, rosemary and pinenuts for a few minutes until just cooked. Place the cooked veal in a bowl and add marjoram leaves, minced cloves of garlic and egg yolk. Season with salt and pepper and mix well.

◉ Cut the iceberg leaves into 20 squares big enough to wrap small balls of the veal mixture. Place the packages in an oven dish and bake in a preheated 180C oven for 15 minutes. Remove from the oven and divide among four bowls. Add a ladle of seasoned chicken broth to each and sprinkle with freshly grated parmesan.

Serves 4

Summer salad of iceberg, rocket and smoked trout

INGREDIENTS

1 head of iceberg, well washed and dried

1 bunch large, spicy rocket, well washed and dried

300g hot smoked river trout, flesh removed from bones in bite-sized pieces

4 anchovy fillets, drained and chopped into small pieces

1 tbsp seeded mustard

4 tbsp extra virgin olive oil

1 tbsp red wine vinegar

salt and pepper

METHOD

◉ Cut the iceberg lettuce into strips about 1cm wide and put into a bowl. Add the rocket, cut into bite-sized lengths along with the pieces of smoked trout and anchovy.

◉ Mix the mustard, olive oil and vinegar in a separate bowl.

◉ Season the lettuce and fish, and then toss with the dressing.

Serves 4

LIMES

Lemons are the citrus fruit commonly used to add acid to food in subtropical regions throughout the world, but the most prominent in the tropics is the lime.

The two are rarely interchangeable because they have a different flavour profile. A lime has 1½ times more acid, weight for weight, than a lemon. This acid adds wonderful flavour to sweet dishes, but less known is lime juice's ability to "cook" protein, especially fish and shellfish. When scallops, for example, are cooked using heat, the protein fibres are "denatured" or broken down. The acid in limes has a similar effect when scallops are marinated in lime juice.

There are various types of lime – sweet (Palestinian or Indian) and sour (kaffir or makrut) – but the two most commonly available are the acidic key lime and Tahitian lime. Both have a glossy green peel but, if left to ripen further on the tree, that skin turns yellow.

Limes go with

Extra virgin olive oil; almond oil; avocado oil; cream; custard; pastry; rice; pasta and noodles; fish sauce; fish paste; sugar; coconut milk; green mango and papaya; chillies; bean sprouts; wok-fried eggs; most fruits, especially coconut, pineapple and melons; fish and crustaceans; beef; duck and quails.

Melon and blueberries with honey-lime dressing

INGREDIENTS

1 small watermelon
1 cantaloupe or rockmelon
1 honeydew
⅓ cup honey
¼ cup lime juice
2 tbsp lemon juice
2 tbsp orange juice
½ tbsp finely grated ginger
½ tsp cardamom seeds
2 tbsp almond oil
2 cups fresh blueberries
chopped mint

METHOD

- This recipe is adapted from *The Art of Indian Vegetarian Cooking* by Yamuna Devi.
- Cut each melon in half, remove the seeds and, using a melon baller, scoop out balls of flesh into a large bowl. Mix well and refrigerate for at least 2-3 hours.
- Meanwhile, in a blender, put honey, lime juice, lemon and orange juice, grated ginger, cardamom seeds and almond oil. Blend to a smooth sauce. Just before serving, drain the melon balls of any liquid and mix them with fresh blueberries. Place in individual bowls and pour the sauce over them. Finish with chopped mint.

Serves 6

Scallop ceviche

Lime mousse

INGREDIENTS

1½ tsp powdered gelatine

3 tbsp cold water

3 eggs

65g caster sugar

250ml cream

90ml lime juice

grated peel from 2 limes

METHOD

◉ Sprinkle the gelatine in the cold water in a saucepan. Whisk the eggs and sugar together till they are pale and hold shape. Whip the cream separately to form firm peaks. Fold the egg and sugar mixture into the whipped cream.

◉ Heat the pan with the gelatine and water gently until the gelatine dissolves. Slowly add the lime juice and peel to the gelatine whisking constantly.

◉ Add the egg-sugar mixture to the juice-gelatine mixture whisking energetically to stop lumps from forming.

◉ Place into individual serving glasses or bowls and refrigerate overnight. Serve with finger biscuits.

Serves 6-8

INGREDIENTS

16 scallops in their shells

13 limes

3 shallots or 1 medium red onion, chopped

2 ripe tomatoes, finely chopped

3 or more chillies, chopped

1 bunch coriander, roughly chopped

4 tbsp extra virgin olive oil

salt and pepper

METHOD

◉ Choose scallops in their shells, which make perfect saucers for serving. Slice each scallop into two or three discs. Slice each disc into four or five strips and place in a bowl. Juice 10 of the limes and add. Mix well. Refrigerate for an hour.

◉ Meanwhile, put chopped shallots or red onion into a bowl. Add ripe tomatoes, chillies and coriander. After the scallops have marinated, strain the lime juice and discard.

◉ Add the scallop strips to the rest of the ingredients and dress the lot with the juice of remaining three limes, extra virgin olive oil, salt and pepper. Toss well, place in the scallop shell or in iceberg lettuce leaves and serve.

Serves 4 as a starter

PICKLES

If you want to see how people express their identity through food, there's no better example than the pickle. It's a way of preserving not only vegetables but also fruit, meat and fish using acid or salt. It is one of the great pre-refrigeration inventions that have taken root throughout the world.

The principle is simple enough: immerse the food in vinegar, salt or a mixture of the two and the nasty bugs don't get a chance to grow. The acetic acid in vinegar is particularly effective compared with other acidic solutions, such as lemon or lime juice, because it acts as a disinfectant.

Cured olives are regarded as a pickle. They are prepared using brine and are naturally fermented by the presence of bacteria, which produces lactic acid. Among similar fermented pickles are Japanese pickled daikon, German sauerkraut, Russian beetroot for borscht and Korean kim chi.

Sugar is sometimes used with salt and vinegar for its sweetness as well as its preserving quality. These are the pickles, chutneys and relishes that need a little sweetness because of their fruit content.

Summer is the time to pickle fruit and vegetables, as they are plentiful and inexpensive.

Maria Cipri's pickled eggplant

INGREDIENTS

as many eggplants as you want to preserve
salt
white wine vinegar
garlic
basil leaves
extra virgin olive oil

METHOD

- Peel eggplant then cut from top to bottom in 5mm-thick slices. Cut slices again in 5mm-wide straws. Toss eggplant straws in fine salt (allow a good pinch per medium eggplant) until well covered. Place in a container, pressing down with a heavy weight so that their water is drawn out. Let sit for 24 hours.
- Take eggplant, squeezing out excess water, and wash off salt with white wine vinegar. Soak for about 5 hours in vinegar, completely submerged, then squeeze eggplant really well and pat dry. Toss with thin slivers of garlic (allow one clove per eggplant) and basil leaves (five medium-sized leaves per eggplant), then store in a glass jar covered with extra virgin olive oil. Keep in a cellar or cool pantry. Lasts at least a year.

Pickles go with
Cured meats such as prosciutto, pancetta, lardo, capocollo, soppressa and the many salami available; terrines such as pork, rabbit and veal; rillet of duck or pork; pâté; antipasto; cold lamb, veal or roast beef; buffalo mozzarella; parmesan; pecorino; chutneys and relishes.

Italian-style pickled vegetables

Pickled red onions

INGREDIENTS

4 litres white wine vinegar

2 litres water

200g sugar

220g salt

5 whole peppercorns

5 whole chillies

5 juniper berries

5 whole cloves

5 bay leaves

2kg cauliflower, trimmed into
small florets

2kg green beans, trimmed and
cut into 3-4cm lengths

2kg carrots, peeled and cut into
3-4cm sticks, 1cm thick

2kg small pickling onions,
peeled and cut in half

METHOD

◉ Place ingredients, except for vegetables, in a large pot and bring to boil. Turn down to a simmer and add vegetables, poaching for 2-3 minutes until tender but still slightly crunchy. Each vegetable will take a different amount of time depending on thickness. As each is ready, remove from simmering liquid with sieve and place in large bowl or plastic container.

◉ Once vegetables are done, mix well in the bowl. Distribute into sterilised preserving jars, cover with hot liquid and follow the manufacturer's instructions on how to seal. Alternatively, the vegetables can be stored, under the liquid, in a sealed container in the refrigerator. They are ready to use after five days.

◉ To serve, simply drain a small quantity and toss with extra virgin olive oil and chopped parsley.

Serves 20

INGREDIENTS

4 large red onions

250ml red wine vinegar

50g sugar

125ml water

METHOD

◉ Peel the onions and cut them each in half. Slice each half into very thin slices. Place the sliced onions in a wide shallow, preferably ceramic, dish. Bring the vinegar, sugar and water to the boil in a saucepan and immediately pour the boiling liquid onto the onions. Let cool to room temperature. They are now ready to be drained and used or, stored in their liquid, they will become tastier over a few days.

◉ To serve, drain, dress with extra virgin olive oil and season as an accompaniment to grilled meats or seafood, or as an addition to summer salads.

Serves 6

CLAMS

Clams have made their way into Australia's kitchens. It wasn't always like this. Thirty years ago clams were used mostly as fishing bait. It was rare to see any available for purchase in fish markets. Now that's all changed.

Even a good suburban fish shop has a decent range of clams such as pipis, vongole and occasionally surf clams. The small cold-water species such as the elaborately patterned vongole are tender and sweet, but larger clams shouldn't be overlooked.

As with most shellfish, overcooking can make them tough. It is often sufficient to steam them till their shells open.

They can then be eaten simply prised from their shell or mixed with other ingredients into a salad of witlof, tomato and avocado, and dressed with vinaigrette. They are particularly good with spinach, lightly fried in olive oil with garlic, and excellent in a Thai hot-and-sour soup.

Expatriate Australian chef David Thompson makes a great clam salad by tossing cooked clams with some sliced red shallots, finely shredded young ginger and dressed with fish sauce and lime juice.

Clams go with
Butter; extra virgin olive oil; sesame oil; XO sauce; soy sauce; chilli; pepper; coriander; turmeric; saffron; onions; shallots; garlic; capsicum; tomato; zucchini; eggplant; fried pancetta; pasta; rice; couscous; white wine; brandy; sherry.

Clams with tomato and thyme

INGREDIENTS

½ cup dry white wine
2 leeks, trimmed and cut into rounds
2 garlic cloves, minced
1 tbsp fresh thyme
1kg ripe tomatoes, peeled and chopped finely
1kg clams, cleaned of any sand
2 tbsp extra virgin olive oil, for drizzling
salt and freshly cracked pepper

METHOD

◉ Place wine, leeks, garlic, thyme and tomatoes in a large pot and bring to boil. Simmer for 2 minutes then add clams. Place a lid on the pot and turn the heat to high. Shake the pot every 30 seconds and in about 3 minutes or so the clams should have opened – discard any that haven't. Taste for salt and adjust if necessary.

◉ Add pepper and serve in deep bowls. Finish by drizzling olive oil over each bowl.

Serves 4

Sardinian couscous with clams

INGREDIENTS

200g Sardinian couscous*
4 tbsp extra virgin olive oil
1 garlic clove, minced
400g vongole or clams, well washed
½ cup parsley, roughly chopped
1 cup fish stock or water
salt and pepper

* Sardinian couscous, or fregola, is larger than Moroccan couscous and is wonderfully chewy with a texture more like pasta.

METHOD

◉ Cook the couscous, like pasta, by plunging in boiling, salted water for 5 minutes. Meanwhile, heat the olive oil in a pan and lightly fry the garlic for 30 seconds. Add the clams and a ladle of the couscous cooking water and turn the heat to high. Cover the pan and shake for 2-3 minutes till the clams open. Remove from the heat and strain the liquid through a double layer of cheesecloth.

◉ Remove the meat from the open clam shells and put back in a pan with the strained liquid. Add the parsley and the strained couscous together with a cup of boiling fish stock or water. Simmer for 15-20 minutes till the liquid has been totally absorbed and the couscous is creamy.

◉ Season to taste with salt and pepper and serve.

Serves 4

Clams with beans

INGREDIENTS

500g dried beans (cannellini, butter or lima), soaked
   overnight in plenty of cold water

1 garlic clove

1 bay leaf

1 small onion, peeled and cut in half

4 sprigs flat leaf parsley, tied together with kitchen twine

pinch saffron threads

3 tbsp breadcrumbs

400g clams – vongole, surf clams, venus clams,
   cockles or even pipis

salt

3 tbsp extra virgin olive oil, for drizzling

METHOD

- This recipe has been adapted from Simone and Ines Ortega's new book of Spanish food, *1080 Recipes*, published by Phaidon.
- Drain and wash beans, put them in a saucepan, cover with cold water and bring to boil. As soon as they boil, drain and return to pot, adding garlic, bay leaf, onion and parsley. Cover generously with cold water. Simmer gently with lid on for an hour, adding more water if needed. Add saffron and stir in. Sprinkle breadcrumbs on the surface of the beans and simmer for 30 minutes more or until tender.
- Meanwhile, wash the clams well, discarding any with broken shells. Place into a pot or frypan, add a cup of water and cook over high heat, with a lid, shaking, until the clams open. Discard any that aren't open and separate the liquid, straining it through a fine sieve, then 15 minutes before serving, mix the clams and their liquid with the beans, heat, season with salt and drizzle olive oil on top.

Serves 4-6

BLUEBERRIES

The blueberry used to be an exotic fruit in Australia. It was introduced in the 1970s from America, using cold-climate varieties so the season was rather short. Some years later, newer, warm-climate varieties were introduced to northern NSW and the industry blossomed.

Native Americans ate blueberries fresh from the bush but also put them out in the sun to dry for winter use. Dried berries were ground to a powder and mixed in with porridge and stew. Wild, low-bush varieties still grow in some parts of north-eastern North America and are carefully tended and protected by locals for their small, intensely sweet fruit.

Commercial varieties in Australia tend to be the high-bush types with larger and easier to pick berries. Look for firm, unwrinkled fruit. There's nothing worse than soft blueberries. It's a sign that the fruit is old or overripe. They should explode with a "pop" in the mouth.

Apart from muffins, try them in a tart filled with lemon curd. Lemon and lime both accentuate and add balance to the berry's natural sweetness.

The blueberry is an ideal partner to dairy, whether it's icecream, yoghurt, custard or whipped cream.

A novel way of serving berries is to set them in jelly; either a light-coloured fruit jelly if there are children involved or sauterne or sparkling wine jelly for the grown-ups.

The season starts with small amounts of fruit in June, peaks from October through to December and continues until about March.

I remember when prices would seldom dip below $6 a punnet, even during the summer months. Nowadays blueberries can be bought for $2.50 in peak season.

Blueberry pepper sauce

INGREDIENTS
250ml water
50g sugar
5 whole peppercorns
200g blueberries

METHOD
- Bring the water, sugar and peppercorns to the boil and stir until sugar has dissolved. Add half the blueberries and simmer for 2 minutes. Strain the liquid, keeping the cooked berries apart. Reduce the liquid by boiling until it has halved.
- Put the cooked berries and the rest of the uncooked berries in a small container. Add the reduced liquid and refrigerate until needed. Serve with the semifreddo, vanilla icecream, pancakes, waffles or yoghurt.

Serves 8

Blueberry sorbetto

INGREDIENTS
1kg blueberries
280g caster sugar
2 tbsp lemon juice

METHOD
- This needs an icecream churner to achieve the smooth texture that is a feature of a good sorbetto.
- Place all ingredients in a blender and process to a puree. Strain the seeds if desired and refrigerate the liquid.
- Once cold, place in an icecream churn to make the sorbetto.

Makes about 1 litre sorbetto

Blueberries go with
Cream; yoghurt; mascarpone; clotted cream; custard; fresh goat's curd; pastry; French toast; brioche; panettone; sponge cake; sugar; honey; lemon juice; brandy, especially cognac and armagnac; liqueurs such as grand marnier, Cointreau and Aurum; chilled rosé or light-bodied red wines; light dessert wines, especially Moscato d'Asti and late-picked riesling or semillon.

Blueberry semifreddo

INGREDIENTS

50g unsalted butter

30g caster sugar

3 punnets blueberries

3 tbsp water

2 egg whites

75g caster sugar

200ml thickened cream

METHOD

Melt the butter in a pan. Add caster sugar and cook until lightly caramelised. Add blueberries and stir gently in the caramel. Add the water and mix it in. Allow the mixture to cool. Beat egg whites in a bowl until they form soft peaks. Gradually add the 75g of sugar, beating, until firm, glossy peaks form. Gently fold into the blueberry caramel mixture. Whip the cream until stiff and fold into the blueberry mixture. Spoon into six moulds and put into the refrigerator overnight to set.

When unmoulding, dip the bottom of each mould into hot water and the semifreddo should slip out. Serve with the blueberry pepper sauce.

Serves 6

CHERRIES

Cherry season in 2007 started with a lot of rain. At least it did out at Orange, where Borry Gartrell began picking in early December at his Borrodell on the Mount orchard. Rain at harvest time means that cherries are likely to split and lose their flavour. The fruit in my local shop at that time was soft, bruised and decidedly unappealing.

What a difference a couple of weeks of sunshine can make. Gartrell said that if it had kept raining, the entire crop could have been lost. Instead, it was a bumper crop at Borrodell with between 60 and 80 tonnes of fruit from 6000 trees. Most of the cherries bound for export to Singapore, Hong Kong and Dubai, were large at about 28mm with some jumbos at 32mm, the size of 50-cent pieces.

Cherries are a versatile fruit that can be used in both sweet and savoury preparations. The classic cherry trifle remains one of the most popular sweets, combining cherries set in jelly, sponge cake and custard. In reality, any pastry such as puff, shortcrust or choux and/or cream such as thick pastry cream, whipped cream or icecream will go with cherries.

I like to have a bowl full of them on the kitchen bench, both as a snack and a reminder that summer and Christmas are here.

If you're having problems with deciding on gifts, a 2kg box of the largest, juiciest cherries, wrapped in festive paper and placed under the tree on Christmas morning is sure to surprise and delight.

Cherries go with
Brandy; rosé and light, sweet white wines; port, liquer, muscat and tokay; vanilla icecream; mascarpone; cream; almond; pork, especially ham; game meats such as kangaroo, pigeon, hare and duck.

Pickled cherries with tarragon

INGREDIENTS
1kg cherries
4 cups white wine vinegar
1 cup sugar
1 tsp salt
8 peppercorns
8 sprigs tarragon (small-leaf French is preferable)

METHOD
- The cherries must be firm and free of blemishes. Using scissors, trim each stalk to 1cm. Wash and dry well, making sure they don't bruise. Sterilise eight 500ml preserving jars and lids (read the manufacturer's instructions on how to do this). Place vinegar, sugar, salt and peppercorns in stainless steel or other non-reactive saucepan. Bring to boil and simmer for 4 minutes.
- Meanwhile, place sprig of tarragon and equal amount of cherries in each jar. Fill each with hot syrup, place a preserving lid on each and seal according to the manufacturer's instructions. The cherries can be used after six weeks.
- Pickled cherries can be used as an accompaniment to prosciutto, salami, pate and terrine. They are good also with roast duck, venison and kangaroo.

Serves 8

Cherries in red wine with panettone and gelato

Cherries in grappa with mascarpone cream

INGREDIENTS

1kg cherries, pitted

50g caster sugar

200ml grappa

½ cup mint leaves

2 egg whites

½ tsp vanilla essence

70g caster sugar

300g mascarpone

METHOD

- Place the cherries in a bowl with the 50g of sugar, grappa and mint. Stir well and place in the refrigerator for 3 hours. Every 30 minutes, stir the cherries well.
- Meanwhile, make the mascarpone cream. Whisk the egg whites by hand until soft peaks form. Slowly add the 70g of sugar while still whisking. Once firm peaks form, fold in the mascarpone and vanilla essence to the mixture.
- Serve the mascarpone cream in individual bowls with the cherries and some of the juice on top.

Serves 8

INGREDIENTS

500g cherries, pitted

750ml red wine

1 cup sugar

1 star anise

2 peppercorns

8 slices panettone, 4cm thick and cut to fit into individual serving bowls

8 scoops vanilla gelato or icecream

METHOD

- Place half the cherries, red wine, sugar, star anise and peppercorns in a pot and bring to boil. Turn down to a simmer for an hour. Strain liquid, discarding star anise and peppercorns. Press juice from cooked cherries and chop up. Reduce liquid by a third and pour, hot, over remaining pitted cherries. Cool before use. The cherries will keep in the refrigerator, in a sealed container, for two weeks.
- To serve, arrange panettone pieces into individual serving dishes. Place some chopped cherries on panettone, scoop gelato on and then spoon some whole cherries and their reduced syrup over the lot.

Serves 8

CORN

The best tasting corn is always going to be the one you grow yourself. That's because, once plucked from the plant, corn converts its sugar into starch at a phenomenal rate. If you can't grow it yourself then it's important to choose corn that's as fresh as possible.

Don't buy corn that has been husked, or even partly husked to reveal the kernels as in those plastic covered trays. It's better to buy each ear loose so it can be inspected. The husks, and the silk underneath (the stringy stuff) give a measure of protection and keep the kernels moist.

Look closely at each ear and feel the kernels beneath. They should be plump. If you want to take a peek at the colour and condition of the corn, fold back a little of the top husk. The kernels should be shiny and full.

Fresh corn should be quickly cooked. If it's on the cob then plunge the whole ear, minus the husk and the silk, into rapidly boiling water for 2 minutes. If the kernels have been taken from the ear, they should be either blanched for 2 minutes or quickly fried. Overcooking can result in the kernels becoming tough.

Butter and good olive oil are the traditional accompaniments but a little roasted sesame oil is excellent. Stir-fry corn kernels with onion, garlic and cumin and then add a chopped tomato. Season and serve as an accompaniment to grilled beef, chicken or fish.

Corn goes with
Butter; extra virgin olive oil; cured meats, especially bacon, pancetta and prosciutto; pork sausages; roast chicken; eggs, especially in an omelette or frittata; cayenne; chilli; fennel; parsley; coriander; thyme; cumin; lemon and lime; spring onions; shallots; garlic; vinegar; red and yellow capsicum; shellfish and crustaceans, especially prawns and crabs.

White corn soup

INGREDIENTS

6 tbsp unsalted butter
1 large white onion, peeled and diced
½ pig's foot (optional)
salt and pepper
5 ears of white corn
nasturtium flowers or chervil

METHOD

- This recipe, from *Chez Panisse Vegetables* by Alice Waters, calls for white corn. Though it has become more widely available of late, yellow corn can be substituted.
- In a deep soup pot put the butter, the onion, the half a pig's foot (a pig's foot imparts a uniquely gelatinous richness to this soup), and a big pinch or two of salt and pepper. Lightly fry over low heat, stirring occasionally, until the onion is very soft and starts to fall apart – about 30 minutes. If the onion begins to dry out and stick to the pan, add a little water.
- While the onion is cooking, slice the corn kernels from the cobs. When the onion is ready, add a litre of water, bring to the boil and add the corn kernels. Simmer for 3-5 minutes until the corn is just cooked. Take from the heat, remove the pig's foot and puree the soup in a blender. Pass through a medium-fine sieve to obtain a uniform, slightly thick texture. Check for salt and pepper and adjust if necessary.
- Serve garnished with chopped nasturtium flowers or chopped chervil.

Serves 4-6

Barbecued corn with tomato, black olive and garlic salsa

Corn and roast cherry tomato salsa

INGREDIENTS

150g cherry tomatoes, washed and each cut in half

sprig each of sage and thyme

3 tbsp extra virgin olive oil

½ cup fresh corn kernels

3 tbsp white wine vinegar

salt and pepper

METHOD

- Place the cherry tomatoes, cut-side up, on a baking sheet. Sprinkle with a tablespoon of the olive oil and season with salt and pepper. Place in a preheated 190C oven for 15 minutes. Remove and let the tomatoes cool to room temperature. Mix them, with any juice on the tray, with the corn kernels and the vinegar. Season to taste.
- Makes an excellent accompaniment to grilled fish or seafood.

Makes about 250ml salsa

INGREDIENTS

250g ripe tomatoes

½ cup pitted black olives, chopped

2 garlic cloves, minced

100ml extra virgin olive oil

juice of 1 lemon

¼ cup roughly chopped flat-leaf parsley

6 ears of corn, still in their husks

salt and pepper

METHOD

- Chop the tomatoes making sure all their liquid, flesh and seeds are collected and put into a bowl. Add the olives, garlic, olive oil, lemon juice and parsley. Season with salt and pepper and leave for at least an hour.
- Prepare the barbecue and cook the corn cobs, still in their husks, for a few minutes then give each a quarter turn. After each turn cook for 2 minutes until each cob has been rotated fully.
- To serve, strip back the husks and the stringy silk. Place on plates and dress with the salsa.

Serves 6

RICE PUDDING

Take a globally prolific staple food such as rice, simmer it in an aromatic liquid with sugar until it is soft and creamy, add a few simple ingredients for taste or texture and the results vary, depending on where rice pudding is made.

Perhaps the simplest – and the one you're most likely to find in small plastic tubs in milk bars and cafes – is the Greek rizogalo. It is made with sweetened milk and a sprinkling of cinnamon. Vietnamese and Cambodian versions consist of sticky white rice cooked in coconut milk and flavoured with banana, mango or jackfruit. India and Pakistan have their varieties of kheer, cooked in milk and flavoured with cardamom and pistachios. In northern India this pudding is sprinkled with fried cashews and raisins and, occasionally, gur (date molasses) is used to sweeten instead of the more modern white sugar. The English are thought to have taken this ancient dish from the subcontinent to eventually produce their own, much loved, rice pudding.

Rice pudding goes with

Cream and clotted cream; custard; brown sugar; maple syrup; rosewater or orange-flower water; citrus peel; dried fruits, especially sultanas, raisins, currants, figs, bananas and apricots; nuts, especially pinenuts, pistachios, almonds, hazelnuts, walnuts and macadamia; vanilla; nutmeg; cinnamon; allspice; star anise; cardamom.

Baked rice pudding

INGREDIENTS

50g ground rice
600ml cold milk
120g caster sugar
125g unsalted butter
4 egg yolks
3 egg whites
25g slivered almonds
50g mixed peel
pinch nutmeg

METHOD

◎ Preheat the oven to 180C. In a saucepan stir ground rice into cold milk until it is smooth. Add caster sugar, stir and bring gently to the boil. Simmer for a minute, add unsalted butter and stir until it has melted.

◎ Turn off the heat, allow it to cool, then mix in four egg yolks. Beat three egg whites until firm, fold into the mixture and add slivered almonds, mixed peel and a pinch of nutmeg. Spoon into a buttered ovenproof dish, and place it in the oven in a water bath with 2cm of water in it. Bake for about 35-40 minutes until firm. Serve hot or cold.

Serves 4-6

Spanish rice pudding

INGREDIENTS

1.5 litres milk
6cm stick of cinnamon
zest of ½ lemon, in large strips
150g Spanish or Italian rice
1 tbsp unsalted butter
120g sugar
pinch salt
ground cinnamon, for dusting

METHOD

◎ This dish is adapted from a recipe in *Seductions of Rice* by Jeffrey Alford and Naomi Duguid.

◎ Place the milk, cinnamon and lemon zest in a pot on a moderate heat. When it is just boiling, stir in the rice and bring back to the boil. Reduce to a very low simmer and cook for 35-45 minutes, until the rice is very soft. Stir occasionally to prevent the rice from sticking. Stir in the butter, sugar and salt. Transfer to individual bowls. Serve warm or cold with a sprinkling of cinnamon.

Serves 6

Italian rice pudding cake

INGREDIENTS

3 cups milk

¾ cup Italian rice (arborio, carnaroli or vialone nano)

4 eggs

½ cup honey

30g pinenuts, toasted

30g macadamias, chopped

30g pistachios, peeled and chopped

30g sultanas, chopped

30g candied citrus peel

1 tsp vanilla essence

grated zest of 1 lemon

2 tbsp unsalted butter, softened

METHOD

Heat milk in a saucepan until it is almost boiling. Add Italian rice (arborio, carnaroli or vialone nano), reduce to a simmer, cover and cook, stirring occasionally, for about 30 minutes until the rice is soft and creamy. Remove from the saucepan and cool. Meanwhile, preheat the oven to 170C. Beat eggs with honey and stir into the cooled rice. Stir in toasted pinenuts, chopped macadamias, pistachios, sultanas and candied citrus peel. Add vanilla essence, the lemon zest and softened, unsalted butter and stir well.

Place in a floured and buttered 25cm cake tin and bake for 50-60 minutes until the cake is set. Cool a little before unmoulding. Keeps well sealed in a container in the fridge for up to a week.

Serves 8-10

PECORINO

Pecorino is one of the few cheeses that can rival parmesan's versatility. When aged, this ewe's milk cheese is as crumbly, easily grated and as distinctively sharp in character as parmesan. Often, especially in central and southern regions of Italy, pecorino is used in place of its more famous northern cousin to grate on pasta dishes, mix into a stuffing or shave on a salad.

Unlike parmesan, however, pecorino comes in many versions. Slow Food's *Italian Cheese*, a guide to 200 traditional types, lists 25 styles across 10 regions. Young pecorino – aged up to six months – can be firm yet creamy. It melts well and with its nutty, even texture is an excellent sandwich cheese and can even be used in a cheeseburger.

At eight months or more, it acquires a rock-like appearance and crumbly consistency. This is when it should be grated, crumbled or shaved and generally used in parmesan's place.

Pecorino goes with
Extra virgin olive oil; vinegar, especially wine, apple cider and sherry; tomatoes; salad leaves; zucchini flowers; braised capsicum; grilled or fried eggplant; capers; asparagus; red onion; spring onions; garlic; basil; oregano; marjoram; parsley; chicken; lamb; pasta, especially lasagne and cannelloni.

Roast tomato, egg and pecorino salad

INGREDIENTS
4 large egg-shaped tomatoes
salt and pepper
1 butter lettuce
4 eggs
6 tbsp extra virgin olive oil
2 tbsp red wine vinegar
1 small garlic clove, finely minced
freshly cracked pepper
½ cup shaved pecorino

METHOD
- Cut tomatoes in half lengthways. Sprinkle the cut side of each with a little salt and pepper and place on a baking tray. Roast in a preheated 160C oven for 15 minutes until they have softened. Remove and cool. Remove the leaves from the butter lettuce and tear into easy-to-eat pieces. Wash well, dry and put into a bowl. Poach (or fry) the eggs so that the yolks are still runny.
- Make a dressing with the extra virgin olive oil, red wine vinegar and finely minced garlic. Toss the lettuce with the dressing, season with salt and freshly cracked pepper and place on a serving platter. Arrange the roast tomatoes in the middle, the poached eggs on top and shaved pecorino scattered over the lot. Sprinkle any leftover dressing on the salad and serve immediately.

Serves 4

Pan-fried lamb cutlets crumbed with pecorino and rosemary

Risotto with pecorino and sage

INGREDIENTS

50g salted butter to start

1 onion chopped fine

500g carnaroli rice

100ml dry white wine

2 litres chicken stock

½ cup sage leaves

salt and pepper

100g salted butter to finish

150g aged pecorino, shaved

METHOD

🍽 In a large, wide pan heat the 50g of butter, add the onions and lightly fry until transparent – do not let them colour. Add the rice and stir until the grains become transparent. Add the wine and stir until it has completely evaporated. Add a ladle or two of boiling stock, simmer and stir until the liquid is almost entirely incorporated. Keep adding the stock a little at a time till almost cooked.

🍽 Remove from heat, add the sage leaves, season with salt and pepper, stir in the butter and pecorino. Rest for 3-4 minutes with lid on before serving.

Serves 6-8

INGREDIENTS

12 lamb cutlets

2 cups breadcrumbs

1 cup grated aged pecorino

handful finely chopped rosemary

pinch salt and pepper

½ cup plain flour

2 eggs, well beaten

3 tbsp extra virgin olive oil

METHOD

🍽 Flatten lamb cutlets by placing each between two pieces of cling film and using a rolling pin with moderate pressure. In a bowl, add breadcrumbs (bread left to dry in a paper bag for a few days on the kitchen bench, then put through a food processor, is best), pecorino cheese, finely chopped rosemary and pinch of salt and pepper. Mix it well.

🍽 Prepare a plate with plain flour, another with the beaten eggs and a third with the crumb mixture. Heat the extra virgin olive oil in a wide frypan. Dust each cutlet with flour first, then coat with the egg and finally the crumbs before frying on both sides until golden. Serve with wedges of lemon.

Serves 4

AVOCADOS

Botanically, the avocado is a fruit but it almost always forms part of our savoury repertoire. While in its native tropical South America avocado flesh is mixed with sugar and eaten as dessert, the rest of the world treats it in much the same way as that other fruit used as vegetable, the tomato.

The avocado's buttery quality comes from a high fat content, a point that is essential in understanding how to use it in the kitchen. Its rich flesh is balanced by the use of acidic accompaniments; the most obvious (and popular) is the classic vinaigrette. The citrus family can also add that tang as lime, lemon and orange can be tossed in a salad as either juice or segments.

Smoked seafood is particularly good with avocado. The most often used is a combination with smoked salmon. But just as good is the less costly hot-smoked river trout. Try flaking the trout and tossing it with some mustard dressing. Fill the avocado's seed cavity with this mixture and finish by sprinkling a few fried capers on top.

The sweet, rich qualities of shellfish such as scallops, mussels and calamari are appropriate to use when a luxurious lunch or dinner is called for. For a grand dish as the weather gets warmer, poach a lobster and slice the tail meat into half centimetre thick medallions. Prepare a mixture of diced avocado, tomato and fennel dressed with extra virgin olive oil and red wine vinegar. Toss it with two or three tablespoons of finely sliced chives and serve the lobster on top.

Avocado salad soup

INGREDIENTS

1 small eggplant

1kg ripe tomatoes, chopped

4 garlic cloves, peeled and chopped

1 tbsp sherry vinegar

2 tbsp fresh basil leaves, sliced

salt and pepper

3 red capsicum

3 avocados

6 asparagus tips, blanched and sliced lengthwise

100ml extra virgin olive oil

METHOD

- This recipe is adapted from Tony Bilson's *Recipe Book*, published in 1987.
- Slice the eggplant into 1cm-wide rounds, salt them, leave for 15 minutes then pat them dry. Fry the slices till golden and drain on absorbent paper then quarter. Pass the tomatoes and garlic through a food mill or puree in a food processor then strain through muslin or a fine sieve. Add the sherry vinegar and the basil. Season with salt and pepper. Roast or grill the capsicum and then peel and slice into strips. Peel the avocados, cut in half and then slice. Arrange in soup bowls with the eggplant slices, capsicum strips and asparagus. Pour over the tomato puree. Drizzle with the olive oil and finish with freshly ground pepper.

Serves 6

Avocados go with

Tomato; onion; garlic; chilli; parsley; chives; thyme; celery; all salad leaves, especially rocket and watercress; cucumber; vinegar; olive, walnut and hazelnut oils; prosciutto; parmesan, pecorino and feta; lemon; lime; chicken; shellfish and crustaceans such as crab, prawns, yabbies and crayfish.

Avocado, tomato, cucumber and bread salad

Avocado with summer herb dressing

INGREDIENTS

2 ripe avocados

1 tsp thyme leaves

¼ cup parsley leaves

¼ cup coriander leaves

100ml extra virgin olive oil

4 tbsp red wine vinegar

salt and pepper

METHOD

 Cut the avocados in half lengthways and remove the skin. Place a half on each of four plates with the cavity facing down. Put the thyme, parsley, coriander, olive oil and vinegar in a food processor and pulse to a thick dressing. Season with salt to taste. If it is too thick, add a little more olive oil. Dress each avocado half, sprinkle with the sliced chives and finish with a couple of turns of pepper.

Serves 4

INGREDIENTS

1 avocado, ripe but not too soft

150g ripe cherry tomatoes

1 Lebanese cucumber, peeled

½ medium-sized red onion, peeled and thinly sliced

100g very dry bread

8 tbsp extra virgin olive oil

4 tbsp apple cider or red wine vinegar

salt and pepper

½ cup roughly chopped parsley

METHOD

Peel the avocado and quarter it. Cut it into 1cm-wide strips and then into similar sized cubes. Put the avocado pieces into a mixing bowl. Cut the cherry tomatoes into quarters and add to the avocado. Cut the cucumber into quarters lengthwise and chop into 1cm wedges. Add to the bowl along with the thinly sliced onion. The bread should be very dry and biscuit-like. Cut it into bite-sized pieces and add it to the rest of the ingredients. Dress with the olive oil and vinegar, season with salt and pepper and toss well. Place in the refrigerator, covered, for an hour. To serve, add the parsley and toss well before arranging on plates.

Serves 4

EGGPLANT

Most other plants in our garden sprout lively green leaves but the eggplant comes from the ground with sinister-looking leaf shades of black and dark green warning of its lineage. Some of its relatives, such as the datura or jimson weed, mandrake, deadly nightshade or belladonna, are poisonous. Don't eat eggplant leaves.

The more unusual eggplant varieties appear in late summer and autumn – the season is in full swing and they are plentiful, flavoursome and inexpensive. Well worth seeking out are the small pea eggplants and the white golf-ball Thai varieties, prized for their bitter-sour flavours and essential in curries and soups. Look also for the slender, mauve-coloured Japanese and the plump, light-purple Italian types. Both are sweet and have tender seeds when fresh.

For a deliciously smoky puree that can be used as a dip, a spread or even an accompaniment for meat or fish, take a plump eggplant and set it directly onto your gas hob or barbecue. Turn it on and char the eggplant skin all over until the flesh feels very soft. Cool a little, scrape out the flesh and mix with lemon juice, a little extra virgin olive oil and your choice of chopped herbs, some smoked paprika, salt and pepper. Mash and serve.

Eggplant goes with

Tomato; zucchini; capsicum; onion; garlic; lemon and lime; chickpeas; beans; capers; anchovies; olives; extra virgin olive oil; bread, especially flatbreads such as ciabatta, roti and Lebanese; chilli; soy sauce; balsamic vinegar; herbs such as parsley, coriander, oregano, mint and basil; cumin; paprika; yoghurt; lamb; chicken; tuna; swordfish; haloumi; parmesan; fresh mozzarella.

Grilled eggplant with roast garlic dressing

INGREDIENTS

2 garlic heads
3 medium-sized eggplants, cut into 1cm slices
2 good pinches salt
juice of 1 lemon
200ml extra virgin olive oil
salt and pepper
20-25 basil leaves

METHOD

Place garlic heads on a tray in preheated 160C oven. They should take 20 minutes or so to soften. Remove, peel and set aside to cool. Salt and wash eggplant slices (see method in next recipe). Meanwhile, make dressing by placing garlic and lemon juice in a food processor and puree. Keep motor running and slowly drizzle in 100ml of the olive oil. The consistency should be thick but just runny. Season to taste with salt and pepper. Brush eggplant slices on both sides with remaining 100ml olive oil. Barbecue or grill, turning once, until cooked through. Set on a platter, scatter basil leaves on top and dress with garlic dressing.

Serves 4

Eggplant slices filled with bechamel

Grilled and marinated eggplant

INGREDIENTS

2 eggplants, washed and sliced into 5mm rounds

100ml extra virgin olive oil

salt

125ml red wine vinegar

2 garlic cloves, peeled

handful of parsley

1 red chilli, seeded

METHOD

- Brush eggplant slices with some of the olive oil, salt and grill on a barbecue or flat grill till golden brown. Place in a tray, side by side, and splash on the vinegar.
- Place the garlic, parsley and chilli on a board and chop together till fine.
- Arrange the eggplant slices in a jar, alternating with the garlic, parsley and chilli mixture. Add the oil to cover the top eggplant slice.
- Seal or cover the jar and leave in the refrigerator for a day or two before using.

Serves 4 as an antipasto

INGREDIENTS

3 medium-sized eggplants, sliced top to bottom about 5mm thick

2 tsp sea salt

200ml extra virgin olive oil

250ml tomato sauce, home-made or store-bought passato

½ cup basil leaves, chopped

Bechamel sauce

250ml milk

30g butter

30g plain flour

4 tbsp parmesan, finely grated

salt and white pepper

METHOD

- Sprinkle eggplant slices with salt and place in a strainer for 30 minutes.
- For the bechamel sauce, heat the milk in a saucepan. In a separate saucepan, melt butter over moderate heat. Whisk in flour and keep cooking until it forms a thick paste. Add warm milk a little at a time and whisk constantly until it starts to boil. Take from the heat and whisk in parmesan and season with salt and white pepper. Set aside to cool.
- Drain eggplant, wash off salt and pat dry immediately with a clean towel. Heat olive oil in a wide pan until it begins to smoke. Fry eggplant slices, turning once, until golden. Drain on absorbent kitchen paper. Roll each slice up with a tablespoon of bechamel and place rolls in an ovenproof dish. Spoon tomato sauce on rolls and sprinkle with chopped basil. Place in preheated 180C oven for 15-20 minutes.

Serves 4

APRICOTS

There are some seasons when flavoursome apricots are hard to come by. When I was growing up, our tree produced good fruit one year in every three, while the figs were as reliable as a Swiss watch.

A bumper apricot crop also means there are plenty of seeds. The hard apricot pit contains the kernel. This seed gives the bitter almond flavour in the amaretto biscuit and liqueur. It can be used to flavour gelati, custards, cakes and jams. It is the essential ingredient in the pumpkin tortellini that are a Christmas fixture in my family.

To extract the kernels, roast the pits in a preheated 180C oven for 15 minutes. Let them cool and, using a nutcracker or a gentle tap with a hammer, extract the kernel. Use them sparingly and store them in a jar in the refrigerator for up to a year.

Apricots go with
Pastry; custards, creams and icecream; sweet wines; vanilla; lemon; orange; almond; pistachio; macadamia; hazelnut; ginger; cinnamon; nutmeg; lamb shoulder stew; coriander; saffron; liqueurs and spirits such as brandy, kirsch, grappa and amaretto; ricotta, clotted cream and mascarpone.

Apricot jam

INGREDIENTS

1.2kg ripe apricots
570g sugar
4 apricot kernels, chopped
juice of 1 lemon

METHOD

- Wash apricots. Pit them (keep the pits) and dice flesh into 1cm cubes. Mix diced apricots with sugar in a large pot and let stand for at least an hour or preferably overnight in refrigerator.
- Add chopped kernels (to extract the kernels, see method in introduction). Bring mixture to boil, stirring so it doesn't catch. It will rise in the pot with large bubbles. Skim off any scum that forms. Lower heat to a vigorous simmer until bubbles get smaller. Test for thickness by placing a few drops on a small cold plate (from refrigerator).
- When ready, remove from heat, stir in lemon juice and place in preserving jars following the maker's instructions.

Makes 2 litres jam

Apricot cream

INGREDIENTS

600g apricots, peeled, stoned and chopped
185g caster sugar
2 gelatine leaves
300ml single cream
1-2 ice cubes, crushed
1 egg white

METHOD

- This recipe is from the Phaidon Press edition of *The Silver Spoon*.
- Put the apricots and 130g of the sugar in a saucepan and cook over a low heat until tender. Meanwhile, fill a small bowl with water and soak the gelatine leaves. Transfer the apricots and liquid to a food processor and puree, then scrape into a bowl. Drain and squeeze out the gelatine, stir it into hot puree and chill.
- Mix cream and ice and beat well. Beat egg white with remaining sugar in a heatproof bowl over a pan of barely simmering water until firm. Allow to cool.
- Mix the three mixtures together and distribute in six serving bowls. Refrigerate for an hour before serving.

Serves 6

Apricot and passionfruit meringue

INGREDIENTS

Poached apricots

10 apricots, ripe but still
    slightly firm

1 litre water

150g sugar

1 tsp vanilla essence

1 tbsp dried jasmine blossoms
    (optional)

Meringue

4 egg whites

pinch salt

¼ tsp cream of tartar

150g caster sugar, divided in
    two equal lots

2 tsp white wine vinegar

1 tsp cornflour

2 tbsp caster sugar, for
    sprinkling on top

300ml double cream, whipped
    with 1 tbsp caster sugar

pulp from 6 passionfruit

METHOD

For the poached apricots, wash well and pat dry. Bring water, sugar, vanilla and jasmine to boil in a pot. Turn down heat and simmer for 2 minutes. Add apricots and simmer for 2-3 minutes, keeping submerged. Remove from liquid, let cool and peel. Cut each apricot in half and remove stone.

For the meringue, preheat the oven to 140C. Whip egg whites with salt and cream of tartar in a mixing bowl until they form soft peaks. Beat in 75g of the sugar, a little at a time, until meringue is stiff and glossy. Fold in the other 75g of sugar as well as vinegar and cornflour, until sugar is well incorporated. Grease and flour a 22cm-tart tin (with removable base). Spoon meringue mixture in and shape the middle flat and the borders slightly higher so that once baked the apricots will sit comfortably in the shallow valley. Sprinkle top with caster sugar and bake for 70 minutes or until a light gold colour and the surface is crusted. Cool on a cake rack before removing. Assemble by spreading a layer of whipped cream on top, followed by apricot halves topped with passionfruit pulp.

Serves 8

OLIVES

Making the olive fruit edible is a long and involved process. It has to be cured to extract the bitter glucosides and the method affects the flavour and texture of the finished olive.

Lye-cured and ash-cured olives are best avoided. This rather harsh treatment softens the flesh and strips the olive of most of its flavour. This type of olive is uniformly jet black and lacks any true olive flavour.

Brine curing is another matter. There, the olives – almost always green – are soaked in a saltwater bath for up to six months. The bitterness is leached out slowly but the flavour is miraculously preserved. Brine-cured olives usually have a smooth, shiny skin and can show differing varietal characteristics.

For most black olives, and for green olives where a crunchier texture is desired, dry salt-curing is the go. The olives are layered with coarse salt in roughly a two-to-one ratio. Every three days they are mixed through the salt and after two months they're washed, dried and preserved in olive oil and aromatic herbs.

Dry-cured olives have a typically wrinkled skin and wonderfully bittersweet flavours.

Olives go with

Extra virgin olive oil; all vinegars, especially wine and apple cider; hazelnut oil; sesame oil; most cheeses, especially fresh mozzarella, parmesan and hard sheep's milk cheeses; tomatoes; roast capsicum; grilled eggplant; cured meats such as prosciutto, jamon, pancetta and coppa; tuna and swordfish; pasta; salad leaves such as iceberg, radicchio and cos; anchovies; capers.

Cucumbers with olives

INGREDIENTS

2 cucumbers, peeled and sliced thinly
salt
1 tbsp chopped dill
1 tbsp lemon juice
1 tbsp extra virgin olive oil
20 black olives, pitted

METHOD

- This recipe is from the Phaidon Press edition of *The Silver Spoon*.
- Put the cucumber slices in a colander, sprinkle with salt and leave them to drain for 30 minutes. Rinse, drain, pat dry and put in a salad bowl. Sprinkle with chopped dill and drizzle with lemon juice and extra virgin olive oil. Add pitted black olives, season with a little salt and toss.
- Let stand for a few minutes before serving.

Serves 4

Roast pork rump with green beans in roast garlic and dried black olives

INGREDIENTS

1kg pork rump
handful of sage leaves
3 garlic cloves, whole
250g green beans, topped and tailed, blanched
100g Italian black dried olives, pitted
3 tbsp extra virgin olive oil
salt and pepper

METHOD

- Prepare the pork rump by scoring the skin in lines with a sharp knife. Rub some olive oil into it, salt it and place on a rack with two sprigs of sage. Roast in a preheated 200C oven for 10 minutes, then turn down to 170C for 45 minutes. Coat the rump with the olive oil and place it in a baking dish or tray on top of a couple of sprigs of sage. Rest it for at least 10 minutes covered with some kitchen foil.
- At the same time roast the garlic cloves whole until they are just soft. Peel each clove and toss with the hot, blanched beans, olives, 3 tablespoons of olive oil, salt and pepper. Slice the rump and distribute among the plates.
- Serve with the beans, garlic and olives.

Serves 6

Chicken with olives

INGREDIENTS

1 large chicken

4 tbsp olive oil

salt

200ml white wine

6 ripe tomatoes, chopped

2 garlic cloves, chopped

2 sprigs thyme

6 sage leaves

1 tbsp marjoram

60g black olives, pitted

8 basil leaves, torn

juice of 1 lemon

METHOD

Cut chicken into pieces, leaving them on the bone and with skin on. Alternatively, use thighs and drumsticks. Heat olive oil in a braising pan. Salt the chicken pieces on the skin side and fry on a moderate heat, turning after 7-8 minutes. Fry both sides until golden brown. Remove the chicken pieces and put them aside in a warm bowl. Add white wine to the pan and turn the heat to high until it all evaporates. Add tomatoes, cloves, thyme, sage leaves and marjoram. Stir well. Once it is bubbling, add the chicken pieces and lower heat to a simmer. Cook for 30 minutes, turning the chicken occasionally. Add black olives and torn basil leaves. Cook for a further 5 minutes and add the juice of a lemon before serving.

Serves 4

CALAMARI

There is often confusion when it comes to squid and calamari. What's the difference? Why is a tub at the fish markets listed as squid and another calamari? What is Hawkesbury calamari and why is it more expensive than all the others? Why don't we use the old English name of "sea clerk"?

The term calamari is reserved for the most highly prized members of the squid family. The difference is in the two flaps or wings on either side of the body. On the calamari, the flaps extend right down the central body tube, while on the arrow squid or pencil squid they are much shorter, like an arrowhead. And when it comes to taste, the calamari is finer-flavoured.

Of the calamari types, the Hawkesbury almost always seems to be the most expensive, although there is some good calamari from Victoria and South Australia. Hawkesbury calamari, contrary to the name, is found in estuaries along the entire NSW coast. It is generally slightly smaller than its southern relatives and a little more delicately flavoured.

Both squid and calamari should be cooked quickly at high heat or slowly braised. Try quick-fried calamari with a simple accompaniment of garlic mayonnaise. Wok-fry strips with thinly sliced garlic and chilli, then serve with a squeeze of lime juice. For something a little more elaborate, the whole calamari tubes can be stuffed with breadcrumbs and herbs then slowly braised in home-made tomato sauce.

Finally, have you worked out why it was called a "sea clerk"? Here's the clue: pen and ink.

Calamari with lemon juice

INGREDIENTS

1 large lemon, cut in half
1 heaped tsp coarse-grained salt
750g calamari, smallest available, cleaned but with tentacles still attached
¼ cup extra virgin olive oil
2 large garlic cloves, peeled and left whole
2 medium-sized carrots, peeled and finely chopped
2 large celery stalks, finely chopped
salt and pepper
large pinch dried chilli flakes
¼ cup clarified chicken stock
juice of 1 lemon
½ cup flat-leaf parsley, coarsely chopped

METHOD

◉ This dish is adapted from a recipe in Giuliano Bugialli's *Foods of Naples and Campania*.

◉ Squeeze lemon halves into bowl of cold water with coarse salt and soak calamari for 30 minutes (put the squeezed lemon halves in as well).

◉ While calamari is soaking, heat oil in a heavy casserole. When it is warm, add garlic cloves and lightly fry for a minute until golden. Add carrots and celery and season with salt, pepper and chilli flakes. Stir.

◉ Drain calamari and rinse well under cold running water. Arrange calamari over the vegetables. Add stock and cook over a very low flame, covered, for 45 minutes. Remove casserole cover, mix well and cook for 2-3 minutes more if there is too much liquid. Add lemon juice and parsley, stir and serve hot.

Serves 4-6

Calamari goes with
Extra virgin olive oil; butter; garlic; onions; chilli; soy sauce; balsamic vinegar; fish sauce; ginger; shallots; spring onions; lime; lemon; tomato; eggplant; zucchini; cucumber; asparagus; beans; peas; all lettuces and leaves, especially rocket, iceberg and cos; mayonnaise.

Calamari with braised spinach and chilli

Spaghetti with calamari and radicchio

INGREDIENTS

4 tbsp extra virgin olive oil

300g cleaned calamari, cut into thin strips

250g radicchio, cut into thin strips

1 garlic clove, minced

200ml dry white wine

handful of parsley, roughly chopped

salt and pepper

400g spaghetti

METHOD

● Heat half the olive oil in a pan and lightly fry the calamari, radicchio and garlic together for a couple of minutes. Add the wine, turn up the heat and evaporate. Season with salt and pepper and add the parsley and remaining olive oil.

● Cook the spaghetti, drain and add to the pan with the calamari and radicchio. Toss well and serve.

Serves 4

INGREDIENTS

2 shallots (or a medium-sized onion), peeled and thinly sliced

2 garlic cloves, minced

2 chillies, sliced

3 tbsp extra virgin olive oil

600g calamari, cleaned and thinly sliced

150g baby spinach, washed

salt and pepper

METHOD

● Fry shallots, garlic and chillies in 2 tablespoons of olive oil until soft. Add spinach and cook until it has just wilted. In another pan, heat remaining olive oil on a high flame and fry calamari quickly for 30-40 seconds, stirring constantly. Add it to spinach and season with salt and pepper. Can be served hot or at room temperature.

Serves 4

AUTUMN

MUSHROOMS

During autumn, Greek, Italian and Lebanese families often go collecting wild mushrooms in the Blue Mountains, maintaining a tradition going back to when people foraged for food. Each family has its own "secret" spot and, of course, their own ways of preparing the mushrooms they find.

A word of warning however: only pick wild mushrooms with someone who knows how to identify the edible species. Ignorance can kill.

Two species grow in abundance in the temperate pine forests. The saffron milk cap, *Lactarius deliciosus*, is a firm-fleshed mushroom. It is orange and bleeds red-orange milk when it is cut or bruised. It is delicious braised or baked whole, sprinkled with olive oil, garlic, parsley and lots of parmesan, in a moderate oven for 10-15 minutes.

The other is the slippery jack, *Suillus luteus*, and its close relation, granulated boletus, *Suillus granulatus*. These are best prepared by peeling the thin, dark-brown skin from the cap and removing the "sponge" underneath. The light yellow flesh is one of the most flavoursome and deliciously textured of all mushrooms. Pan-fry in a little butter with garlic and parsley, then serve on toast.

What to look for

When buying mushrooms, look for freshly cut stems and caps that have bright, even colour. Of the cultivated mushrooms, white buttons should have bright, white caps; shiitake should be firm, full and dry, though not shrivelled; Swiss browns or honey browns should be full and firm with a light buffed-brown cap. Of the wild mushrooms, the saffron milk cap should have a bright-orange cap and gills, with no dark blotches; the slippery jack or pine boletus should be dark amber brown with a dry sponge instead of gills.

Mushrooms go with

Butter and extra virgin olive oil; cream; parmesan, pecorino and goat's cheese; beef; rabbit; chicken; eggs; onions; garlic; spring onions; lemon; toast; wine vinegar; parsley; coriander; thyme; pepper; chilli; wine.

Mushrooms on toast

INGREDIENTS

600g mushrooms
3-4 tbsp extra virgin olive oil
1 onion, finely chopped
3 garlic cloves, minced
½ cup roughly chopped Italian parsley
salt and pepper

METHOD

◉ Cut mushrooms into thin slices. Heat extra virgin olive oil in a pan and fry a finely chopped onion and minced garlic cloves for 30 seconds. Add the mushrooms and stir till they wilt – about 3 minutes. Add roughly chopped Italian parsley, season with salt and pepper and stir. Cook for 5 minutes.

◉ Serve on toast.

Serves 4

Mushroom and bean soup

INGREDIENTS

200g fresh borlotti beans (or 150g dried and soaked overnight)
2 garlic cloves, peeled
1 carrot, peeled and sliced
1 stick celery, washed and sliced
6 tbsp extra virgin olive oil
600g assorted mushrooms, thinly sliced
3 litres vegetable stock or water
80g grated parmesan
salt and pepper

METHOD

◉ Cook the beans in water till tender. Drain and reserve till needed. Chop the garlic, carrot and celery together until finely minced. Heat the olive oil in a pot and fry the mixture together, continually stirring, for 3-4 minutes on a medium heat. Add the sliced mushrooms and stir in, cooking, for another 2-3 minutes. Add the vegetable stock or water and simmer for 45 minutes. Add the cooked beans and simmer for 10 minutes more.

◉ Season with salt and pepper and serve with the grated parmesan.

Serves 4-6

Wild mushroom risotto

INGREDIENTS

1½ litres chicken stock

50g butter

1 onion, finely chopped

500g carnaroli (or arborio) rice

200ml white wine

25g dried porcini mushrooms, soaked in water for a minute, then drained

200g assorted mushrooms, finely sliced

2 pinches salt

100g butter, cut into pieces

²/₃ cup grated parmesan

METHOD

🍽 Place a pot of simmering chicken stock on the stove top. In a wide pan heat butter, add onion and sauté until transparent – about a minute. Add carnaroli (or arborio) rice and stir until the grains are transparent – about 2 minutes. Add white wine and allow it to completely evaporate. Add two or three ladles of the simmering chicken stock, then stir. Add mushrooms. Add chicken stock a little at a time, waiting until it is absorbed before adding more, and stir.

🍽 After 15 minutes (carnaroli rice takes longer than arborio) or so, add a couple of good pinches of salt and taste. It should still be a little chalky. Remove from heat, stir in butter and grated parmesan. Put the lid on and rest for 3-4 minutes.

🍽 Serve with grated parmesan.

Serves 8

PARSNIPS

Most of the time, parsnips are passed over for other vegetables. They're not fashionable or glamorous, looking more like deformed white carrots. And, unlike their close relative the carrot, parsnips are particularly unpalatable raw. Only when cooked – fried, roasted or boiled – is the parsnip's deliciously rich, nutty flavour released.

During the cooler months, parsnip is a particular favourite of mine. No array of roast vegetables is complete without caramelised rounds of it sitting in the baking dish next to the carrots, celeriac and potatoes. Made into a puree, it's a perfect accompaniment to rich beef stews or braises, pork belly or duck confit. The 18th-century doyenne of home cookery, Hannah Glasse, recommended salt cod with hard-boiled eggs and parsnip puree mixed with butter and cream.

Parsnip cakes or fritters make a great snack. Boil pieces of peeled parsnip until soft. Add beaten eggs, breadcrumbs, grated parmesan, salt and pepper. Shape into small, flat cakes. Roll in more breadcrumbs and fry in butter until golden brown.

Parsnips are a vegetable, requiring a good few months to grow. They develop their characteristic sweetness only after prolonged cold weather and frost. Their preparation favours the heartier dishes of the colder months.

Parsnip chips

INGREDIENTS
parsnips
extra virgin olive oil or
    peanut oil
salt

METHOD
- Parsnips can be deep-fried just like potato chips. Peel and cut the parsnips into slices about 2.5mm thick. Pat them dry with a tea towel. Heat extra virgin olive oil or peanut oil in a deep pot to 180C. Fry the parsnip chips until they are golden brown. Drain on paper, salt them well and serve immediately.

Roast parsnips with sage

INGREDIENTS
8 large parsnips
4 tbsp extra virgin olive oil
1 cup fresh sage leaves
3 pinches salt

METHOD
- Peel the parsnips and cut off the woody ends. Cut the parsnips into 1cm cubes and place in a roasting tray. Add the olive oil and sage leaves. Season with three good pinches of salt and mix everything together so the parsnips and sage are well coated with the oil. Place in a preheated 190C oven for 30-40 minutes. Every 10 minutes mix the parsnips well.
- Serve hot as an accompaniment to roasts or use cold as a sandwich or panino filling.

Serves 6

What to look for
Seek firmness and smooth skin. Avoid parsnips that are too large – they will probably have a woody core and not much tender flesh. Medium-sized ones give the best yield. Discard any that are discoloured or damaged.

Parsnips go with
Butter; extra virgin olive oil; cream; garlic; potatoes; peas; carrots; Jerusalem artichokes; leeks; onion; rosemary; thyme; coriander; parsley; duck – roast, grilled or confit; beef – grilled or roast, but especially the secondary cuts such as braised cheek, brisket and tail; pork – prepared any way but especially sausages.

Parsnip soup

INGREDIENTS

1 large leek
8 garlic cloves
100g butter
1 large, floury potato
8 parsnips
chicken stock or water
salt and white pepper
a few slices of salami
extra virgin olive oil
knob of butter

METHOD

◉ Trim the leek, discarding the tough base and thick outer leaves. Wash well and slice into thin rounds. Peel and slice garlic cloves and lightly sauté with the sliced leek in a soup pot with butter, until soft. Take care not to have the heat up too high so that the vegetables don't colour.

◉ Peel the potato. Peel and trim parsnips, removing the core if they are a little old. Slice the potato and parsnips into 1cm-thick pieces and add them to the pot. Cover the vegetables with chicken stock or water and bring to the boil. Turn down the heat and simmer for 30 minutes until the parsnips are soft. Season with salt and fine white pepper, then puree in a food processor. If it's too thick, add a little more stock or water. Slice good salami into fine strips and lightly fry in olive oil until crisp. To finish, add a good knob of butter to the hot soup, ladle into bowls and sprinkle the fried salami on top.

Serves 4

PUMPKIN

Before the time of Columbus, the entire family of squashes, including marrows and pumpkins, was unknown in Europe. It was part of the phenomenal riches brought back from the Americas by the early explorers.

Pumpkins in all shades and sizes grew in North and South America. They were particularly prized because they could be eaten when young and could also be stored, maturing and intensifying in flavour.

Pumpkins' flesh ranges from a pale yellow to a deep, burnished orange and can be used in savoury and sweet dishes. Perhaps the easiest preparation is to steam or boil, then mash it to make a puree or blend it with butter, cream and extra flavouring such as garlic and herbs to make soup. It can also be cut into largish cubes – about 3cm – and tossed in a pan with some butter or extra virgin olive oil until the pumpkin is tender and golden brown – delicious served hot with grilled beef or cold in a salad.

Finish with an old-fashioned Australian gramma pie or American pumpkin pie – both classic desserts.

What to look for
Pumpkin should be firm with no bruises on its skin. It should feel heavy for its size. The Queensland blue should have tough skin – if a fingernail easily pierces the skin, chances are it has not been seasoned. I'm still seasoning my autumn-harvest blues on top of the shed, where they'll get better as they dry. If you are buying pre-cut pieces, as a general rule the deeper the colour, the more intense the flavour.

Pumpkin goes with
Butter; extra virgin olive oil; cream; cheeses such as gruyere and parmesan; herbs such as thyme, rosemary, parsley, sage and tarragon; spices such as pepper, paprika, cayenne, cinnamon, nutmeg and chilli; roast meats, especially lamb and pork; beef stew; brown and black sugars; maple syrup; pecans.

Roast pumpkin soup

INGREDIENTS
1.5kg butternut or Queensland blue pumpkin

extra virgin olive oil

salt and pepper

sprig of thyme

4 garlic cloves, unpeeled

1.5 litres chicken stock

150g butter

METHOD
- Preheat the oven to 190C. Split butternut or Queensland blue pumpkin into two, scraping out seeds and pith. Oil the cut sides with extra virgin olive oil and season with salt and pepper. Place the halves, cut-side down, on a baking sheet with the sprig of thyme and the unpeeled garlic cloves tucked into each cavity. Roast in the oven for 45 minutes or until tender. Remove from oven and cool a little.
- Peel or scoop out the flesh and put it in a soup pot along with the roast garlic, squeezed from its skin. Mash together with a fork or whisk, add chicken stock and bring to a simmer. Check the seasoning, whisk in butter and serve.

Serves 4

Sweet and sour pumpkin with mint

INGREDIENTS

1kg Queensland blue or
    Japanese pumpkin
½ cup extra virgin olive oil
8 garlic cloves, crushed
½ cup chopped mint
½ cup red wine vinegar
⅓ cup sugar
salt and pepper

METHOD

- Peel pumpkin, removing seeds and pith. Cut it into 8cm lengths with a thickness of 1cm. Heat extra virgin olive oil in a wide pan, sauté cloves of crushed garlic until golden, discard and turn up the heat. Fry the pumpkin slices in batches and on both sides until tender. Lay slices on a deep platter and sprinkle with chopped mint.
- Add red wine vinegar and sugar to the olive oil. Turn up the heat and boil until the mixture thickens slightly. Pour it over the pumpkin, season with salt and pepper and marinate for 3 hours. Serve at room temperature.

Serves 8

Venetian-style pumpkin

INGREDIENTS

1kg pumpkin
100g plain flour
150ml extra virgin olive oil
200ml white wine vinegar
2 garlic cloves, peeled and crushed
2 pinches salt and pepper
1 cup basil leaves

METHOD

- Prepare the pumpkin by removing the seeds and skin. Slice the pumpkin into 5mm pieces. Lightly flour each piece and fry on both sides in a pan with the olive oil. Remove the fried pumpkin and drain on a tray with absorbent paper.
- Bring the vinegar and garlic to the boil in a pot and season with a couple of pinches of salt and pepper. Boil for 5 minutes then turn off. In a ceramic container or dish, layer the bottom with a stratum of fried pumpkin. Scatter some basil leaves and then another layer of pumpkin. Repeat until the pumpkin has all been used.
- Pour the hot vinegar and garlic mixture over the pumpkin. Let it cool before covering and placing in the refrigerator for 24 hours.
- To serve, remove from the vinegar and dress with olive oil, salt and pepper.

Serves 4

SWORDFISH

A number of people have told me they don't eat swordfish because the fish mate for life and, after all, why eat such majestic animals? Well, we eat many animals that are majestic – or cute and cuddly for that matter: veal, fluffy bunnies, kangaroo and venison come quickly to mind.

Swordfish, I'm relieved to report, probably aren't loving, monogamous life partners. Unlike tuna, which congregate in schools, swordfish are solitary predators and only come together during spawning season between October and May.

There seems to be an increasing number of us eating swordfish, especially in our cities, and it's easy to see why. The texture of its flesh is fine and not overly fishy. Its not-too-dominant flavour means it's a great carrier for other, more assertive partners such as lemon and lime, chilli and olives. And swordfish is user-friendly. Because it is usually available in cutlets "off the bone", there are no bones to worry about.

Swordfish catches in Australia have been increasing steadily – from 50 tonnes a year taken in 1994 to 3800 tonnes in 1999. Local markets for swordfish have grown but, more crucially, Japan and the US are increasingly taking more of the catch as their own swordfish populations dwindle. It's not yet a protected species in Australia because, to date, we haven't overfished it, but it's being watched to make sure it's sustainable.

Grilled swordfish steaks

INGREDIENTS

180g swordfish steak per person

1 cup chopped flat-leaf parsley

¼ cup extra virgin olive oil

3 garlic cloves, minced

salt and pepper

METHOD

🍽 Allow 180g of swordfish, 2cm thick, per person. Make a dressing with chopped flat-leaf parsley, extra virgin olive oil, minced garlic cloves, salt and pepper. Sit the swordfish steaks in this dressing for a couple of minutes. Cook on a hot grill for a minute on each side. Remove and spoon remaining dressing on the steaks.

🍽 Season and serve with lemon and a Greek or simple leaf salad.

Makes dressing for 8

What to look for

Swordfish fillets are far too large to handle so the steak is the usual cut. At the fish market or at a good fishmonger, a side of swordfish is displayed on a table. You indicate the thickness and quantity of steaks you want and the fishmonger will cut it for you. The flesh should be pale white to pink with a prominent bloodline near the bone.

Swordfish goes with

Lemon and lime; butter and extra virgin olive oil; herbs, especially coriander, parsley, fennel, basil, oregano and rosemary; spices such as cumin, paprika, cayenne pepper, fennel seeds and black pepper; chilli; garlic; fish sauce; soy sauce; sambal; vinegar; capers; olives; salad leaves, especially the tangy/bitter ones like sorrel, rocket, radicchio and endive.

Swordfish tagine

INGREDIENTS

1 red onion, finely chopped

½ cup coriander leaves

½ cup Italian parsley, roughly chopped

2 garlic cloves, minced

3 tsp ground cumin

4 tsp paprika

2 tsp turmeric

1 tsp cayenne pepper

1 tsp ground black pepper

2 tsp salt

1 onion

3 zucchini

2 waxy potatoes

2 ripe tomatoes

1 red capsicum

½ cup water

500g swordfish

4 tbsp red wine vinegar

METHOD

🍽 A tagine is a Moroccan earthenware cooking implement as well as the dish prepared inside it (pictured). A casserole dish with a lid will also do the job.

🍽 Mix together red onion, coriander leaves and Italian parsley, garlic cloves, ground cumin, paprika, turmeric, cayenne pepper, ground black pepper, salt.

🍽 Chop into bite-sized chunks: onion, zucchini, waxy potatoes, ripe tomatoes and red capsicum. Toss the vegetables in the spice mix and place in the dish. Add water, cover and place on a very low heat. Cook for 45 minutes. Cut swordfish into pieces 2cm thick by 5cm long. Add red wine vinegar to the vegetables, and then lay the swordfish on top. Cover and turn off the heat. After 5 minutes, serve with couscous or rice.

Serves 6-8

Swordfish with red onions

INGREDIENTS

4 tbsp extra virgin olive oil

2 large red onions, peeled and thinly sliced

200ml red wine

1 tbsp butter

4 swordfish steaks about 200g each

2 garlic cloves, peeled and crushed but left whole

1 tbsp grappa or brandy

½ cup parsley, roughly chopped

salt and pepper

METHOD

🍽 Heat the olive oil and lightly fry the onions for 3-4 minutes till transparent. Add the red wine and simmer till the onions are creamy and all the liquid has been absorbed or evaporated. In a wide pan heat the butter and fry the swordfish steaks on both sides for a minute. Add the garlic and flame by adding the brandy. Keep lightly frying for a couple of minutes more then add the onion. Cook for 2 minutes more until all the onions have been scattered evenly on each steak. Add the parsley, season with salt and pepper and serve.

Serves 4

TOMATOES

In Bunol, an agricultural village near Valencia, Spain, the locals indulge in a yearly event that lasts only 15 minutes but can take weeks to clean up. On the last Wednesday in August, people take part in La Tomatina, a festival thought to have originated when a cart carrying ripe tomatoes overturned in the village centre.

Tonnes of tomatoes are brought into town and emptied into the streets. In the ensuing 15 minutes, participants cover everything in sight with red pulp. The dictator Franco found it all a bit too much and, in 1935, banned the event. After he died, La Tomatina was revived.

Today, the tomato is an indispensable ingredient in our cuisine – from a salad made with a firm, green-red oxheart to a pungent, aromatic sauce coaxed and cooked from the deep-red, elongated Roma (San Marzano). More and more, we can buy tomatoes with flavour as growers and merchants realise that taste is all-important. More recently, sprays of small truss tomatoes, still on their branch, have been easier to find. These are perfect for roasting "on the vine" with a little good olive oil and some sea salt.

Bruschetta with tomato and chilli

INGREDIENTS
sourdough or rustic bread, cut into 1cm-thick slices
1 garlic clove
4 tbsp good extra virgin olive oil
3-4 salad tomatoes
4 tbsp fresh oregano leaves
1-2 chillies, thinly sliced
juice of ½ lemon
1 tbsp extra virgin olive oil
salt and pepper

METHOD
- Allow a 1cm-thick slice of good sourdough or rustic bread per person. Mince a clove of garlic into a small dish with the good extra virgin olive oil.
- Brush both sides of the bread slices with the garlic oil and grill lightly. Dice salad tomatoes into a bowl. Add fresh oregano leaves, thinly sliced chillies, the juice of half a lemon and the tablespoon of extra virgin olive oil. Season with salt and pepper, and mix well.
- Spoon onto the toasted bruschetta and serve.

Serves 4

What to look for
Selecting tomatoes depends on their eventual use. For use in a sauce, look for full, deep colour and a soft texture and smell for flavour. An Oxheart destined for a salad should be firm and half green, half red. Fully ripe Oxhearts are floury. Never put tomatoes in the fridge, they stop ripening. You'll find they can live happily in a bowl on the kitchen table.

Tomatoes go with
Bread, toasted or fresh; herbs, especially basil, oregano, thyme, parsley, coriander and chives; onions, shallots and garlic; ginger; chilli and capsicum; soft cheeses such as triple cream, brie and goat's curd; firm cheeses such as parmesan and cheddar; mustard; salad leaves; cucumber; sea salt; pepper; vinegar, especially wine, balsamic and apple cider.

Spaghetti with fresh tomato and basil sauce

INGREDIENTS

8 tbsp extra virgin olive oil

2 onions, minced

3 garlic cloves, minced

3kg fresh Roma tomatoes, pureed

1 bunch of basil leaves, roughly torn

salt and pepper

spaghetti

METHOD

🍽 Heat extra virgin olive oil in a saucepan and gently fry minced onions and minced garlic cloves until they have softened, about 2-3 minutes. Add pureed, fresh Roma (San Marzano) tomatoes, stir well and simmer for 40 minutes. Add a bunch of roughly torn basil leaves, season with salt and pepper, and simmer for a further 5 minutes. Cook the spaghetti al dente, drain and toss with some of the tomato sauce. Serve with plenty of freshly grated parmesan.

Makes 4 litres sauce

Roast tomatoes with buffalo mozzarella and pesto

INGREDIENTS

6 ripe tomatoes

6 tsp extra virgin olive oil

1 cup fresh basil leaves

60g pinenuts, toasted

2 medium-sized garlic cloves, peeled

½ cup extra virgin olive oil

6 tbsp grated parmesan

mixed salad leaves

6 slices of buffalo mozzarella

salt and pepper

METHOD

🍽 Take a sharp knife and remove the woody part of each of the tomatoes at the stem end. Cut into the flesh for 2cm. Place the tomatoes on a baking tray and preheat the oven to 180C. Pour a teaspoon of extra virgin olive oil into each cavity you've made. Season with salt and pepper and roast for 10-15 minutes or until the tomato has softened and is tender without having split. Remove and set aside.

🍽 In a mortar place the basil leaves, pinenuts, garlic and a good pinch of salt. Pound until everything has broken down to a paste. Add the half cup of extra virgin olive oil, mixing, to give the desired consistency. Mix in the parmesan and adjust seasoning if necessary.

🍽 Assemble the dish starting with a bed of mixed salad leaves, then a slice of buffalo mozzarella and then the roast tomato. Finish by drizzling plenty of pesto over the dish and serve.

Serves 6

PEARS

I once visited a very clever gardener, in a suburb of Melbourne, whose backyard was a paradise of things to eat. The plot was of ordinary size but it was a lesson in utilisation of space and rarely did his family have to buy produce from a fruit shop.

The cleverest use of space was an unusual fruit tree. It had limbs with different varieties of apples and pears. He did this by grafting, made possible because the botanical difference between apples and pears is literally a hair's breath or, more technically, the separation of their pistil stems.

Similarly, in the kitchen, pears and apples can be successfully interchanged in dishes. While apple and roast pork is a classic combination, try slicing and roasting crisp, firm-fleshed pears as an alternative and sprinkling with your favourite vinegar. Classic also is the combination of a not-too-ripe packham or williams pear and aged parmesan.

Williams and packham make up the lion's share of varieties grown in Australia. They can be eaten fresh, used in salads and even baked if not too ripe. The russet and yellow-skinned bosc is a little more versatile. It's a good pear to poach in either white or red wine with a little cinnamon, star anise or even peppercorns.

When in season, it's well worth harassing your fruiterer about the lesser-known varieties. Winter neils are a small, super sweet variety, good for poaching whole and preserving. The josephine has great flavour and can be either eaten fresh or cooked. My favourite of all is the rarely seen and late maturing comice. Enjoy this one as a fresh piece of fruit.

Perth honeyed pears

INGREDIENTS

6 pears, any type
¼ cup honey
1 cup orange juice
¼ cup lemon juice
¾ cup water
1 stick cinnamon 5-6 cm long
2 cloves

METHOD

- From *The Australian Honey Recipe Book* published in 1973.
- Peel the pears, leaving the stalks attached. Place them in a saucepan. Combine the honey, orange juice, lemon juice, water and spices, and bring to the boil. Pour over pears. Put lid on saucepan and simmer gently until cooked (test with a sharp knife or skewer). Baste pears from time to time with the syrup as they cool. Serve with whipped cream.

Serves 6

Pears with vanilla cream

INGREDIENTS

2 ripe pears, packham or williams
1 vanilla bean
60g caster sugar
150ml fresh cream

METHOD

- Keep the pears in the refrigerator for at least 3 hours. When cold, cut each in half and scoop out a neat cavity where the core and seeds are. Peel each half carefullly and return to the refrigerator.
- Meanwhile, split the vanilla bean in half lengthways and scrape the seeds into the sugar. Mix well. Whip the cream with the vanilla sugar until it forms firm peaks. Spoon a little of the cream into each pear cavity (there should be a little cream remaining). Place the pears in the freezer for an hour and the leftover whipped cream in the refrigerator. To serve, place a dollop of whipped cream in the centre of each serving plate and sit each pear half on top.

Serves 4

Pears go with
Spices such as cloves, cinnamon, nutmeg, pepper, anise; ginger and cardamom; honey and sugar; butter; custard; cream; vanilla; maple syrup; passionfruit; almonds, macadamia and walnuts; parmesan and pecorino; duck; goose; quail.

Butterscotch pears with aniseed praline

INGREDIENTS

Praline

140g sugar

30ml light corn syrup

30ml water

1 tbsp unsalted butter

½ tsp baking powder

pinch salt

1 tbsp aniseed

Pears

6 pears, peeled (josephine, bosc or comice)

200g sugar

60g unsalted butter

8 tbsp water

METHOD

🍽 For the praline, combine the sugar, water, corn syrup and butter in a saucepan. Cook over medium heat until the mixture is a light caramel colour. Remove from heat and quickly whisk in the baking powder, salt and aniseed. With a buttered spatula spread the mixture quickly onto a non-stick baking sheet. Cool completely. Store in an airtight container between sheets of greaseproof paper. Grind as needed in a mortar or food processor.

🍽 For the pears, preheat the oven to 170C. Place the sugar in an ovenproof saucepan wide enough to hold the pears. On a moderate heat, cook the sugar to a caramel colour but not too dark. Carefully add the butter and whisk. Add the pears and lightly cook in the butterscotch, constantly turning, for 2-3 minutes. Add the water and spoon the liquid over the pears until well basted. Transfer the pan to the oven and bake till tender (about 15-25 minutes depending on size). Baste every 5 minutes. They are done when a sharp knife easily pierces the pear. Serve warm or at room temperature with some cooking liquid and the ground praline.

Serves 6

CAULIFLOWER

The celebrated American chef Paul Bertolli says in his book *Cooking by Hand* that he doesn't much like cauliflower. He elaborates by calling it "dry and gritty" and says it "resists the improvement of even strong dipping condiments".

Alice Waters, founder and proprietor of the famed restaurant Chez Panisse in Berkeley, California, and Bertolli's one-time employer, has a different perspective. She likes to serve sweet, fresh cauliflower very simply, "perhaps with bagna cauda; steamed and served with brown butter, parsley, sieved egg and breadcrumbs; or as a smooth cream of cauliflower soup".

For me, the subtlety of cauliflower is its strength. I love the mild pepperiness that is a feature of all the brassica family – cabbage, broccoli, brussels sprouts and kale. And as long as it's not overcooked, its subtle features hold up even when strong spices are used.

The last word goes to Waters: "The mildness of cauliflower is also good when set against other more assertive flavours. In the winter, its colour and freshness make cauliflower a welcome part of an antipasto. One of our favourite pastas combines cauliflower with garlic, anchovies, olive oil and hot pepper flakes."

Cauliflower goes with

Cheeses, especially cheddar, parmesan and gruyere; onion; leek; garlic; broccoli; braised lentils; lemon; curry; chilli; butter; extra virgin olive oil; sesame oil; rice; pasta; olives; capers; parsley; thyme; coriander; cumin; toasted sesame seeds; turmeric; walnuts; almonds; anchovies.

Pickled cauliflower

INGREDIENTS

450g cauliflower florets
1 garlic clove, peeled
200g peeled small onions
1 bay leaf
sprig of thyme
1 chilli
2 cups tarragon vinegar
1 tsp sea salt

METHOD

◉ This recipe is adapted from *Chez Panisse Vegetables* by Alice Waters.

◉ Place cauliflower florets, peeled garlic clove, peeled small onions, bay leaf, sprig of thyme and chilli in a hot, sterile preserving jar.

◉ Bring tarragon vinegar and sea salt to the boil and boil for a minute. Pour it over the cauliflower, which should then be covered with vinegar. If it isn't, simply boil more vinegar to top it up. Secure the lid and let the jar stand to cool. Store it in a cool, dark place for a month before using.

◉ Then, drain the cauliflower and dress with a little olive oil, season with salt and pepper and toss with some chopped chilli and parsley. It's delicious as part of an antipasto with olives and dried tomatoes.

Serves 6

Cauliflower soup with gruyere crostini

INGREDIENTS

2 tbsp extra virgin olive oil

1 onion, finely chopped

2 garlic cloves, minced

650g cauliflower, cut into small florets

750ml water

salt and ground white pepper

1 baguette

grated gruyere or cheddar

METHOD

🍽 Heat extra virgin olive oil in a pot. Add finely chopped onion and minced garlic cloves. Fry gently for 5-6 minutes. Add cauliflower florets and water. Simmer until the cauliflower is tender. Season with salt and ground white pepper and puree until very smooth. Let it sit for 30 minutes to thicken.

🍽 Meanwhile, cut some slices of baguette a 5mm thick and toast them lightly. Place a little grated gruyere or cheddar on each piece and grill until it melts. Serve with the hot soup and finish with a drizzle of olive oil.

Serves 4

Cauliflower patties

INGREDIENTS

1 cauliflower head, about 700g in weight

2 cups water

2 garlic cloves, peeled

1 sprig of mint

¼ cup parsley

2 eggs, beaten

¼ cup breadcrumbs

40g pecorino, grated

40g parmesan, grated

salt and pepper

6 tbsp extra virgin olive oil

METHOD

🍽 Trim the cauliflower of external leaves and put in a pot with the water. Place the pot on a medium flame and bring the water to a boil. Place a lid on the pot and turn the heat down very low. The cauliflower should steam for around 20 minutes till tender. Add more water if needed. Remove, put into a bowl and, while still hot, mash with a fork.

🍽 Finely chop the garlic, mint and parsley together and add to the cauliflower with the breadcrumbs, beaten eggs and the two grated cheeses. Season well with salt and pepper and mix well. Form patties of around 5cm in width. Heat the olive oil in a pan and fry the patties on both sides till golden.

🍽 Serve hot or at room temperature.

Serves 4-6

CHESTNUTS

W e may have embraced the dazzling variety of cuisines brought by waves of migration, but when most of us go into an ethnic shop we're lost in a world of weird and wonderful ingredients and packaging.

Even in the relatively user-friendly Italian deli there are ingredients that can puzzle the curious cook, such as sacks of loose dried broad beans, splayed dried cod hanging on hooks or flour made from grains other than wheat.

You may have come across dried, peeled chestnuts and wondered how these hard little buttons are used. It might help when cooking them to think of chestnuts, both fresh and dried, as a starch rather than a nut. In many cases, chestnuts can be used like potatoes – cooked and chopped in salads, added to soup, peeled and tossed whole in a pan with butter and herbs or cooked in a pie.

Perhaps the simplest way to prepare fresh chestnuts, in season, is to oven roast them. First, make a small cut on one side of the shell. This prevents the nut exploding during cooking as the moisture inside turns to steam. Place the cut chestnuts under a moderate to hot grill for 10-15 minutes depending on the size. Wrap them up for 5 minutes in a tea towel, giving them a little squeeze. Unwrap, peel and eat.

Chestnuts go with
Rice; pasta; gnocchi; ricotta; parmesan; pecorino; onion; garlic; cloves; nutmeg; rosemary; bay leaf; parsley; cauliflower; brussels sprouts; radicchio; leeks; raisins; prunes; apples; cream; sugar and honey; rum, brandy, grappa and marsala; sausages; quail; goose; turkey; duck; pheasant; guineafowl; chicken; pork; venison; rabbit and hare.

Chestnut soup

INGREDIENTS

1kg peeled chestnuts, dried
    or frozen
1 onion, chopped
½ celery head, chopped
1 carrot, chopped
1 small potato, diced
1 ripe potato, chopped
½ bunch parsley
2 cloves
2 veal shanks (optional)
salt and pepper

METHOD

🍽 Take dried or frozen, peeled chestnuts and boil them until tender. Place them in a food processor or "mouli" and work to a paste, adding a little water if necessary. Make a stock by adding onion, celery, carrot, potato, ripe tomato, parsley, cloves and veal shanks (optional) to a large pot, with cold water, and bring to the boil. Turn down to a simmer for 2 hours then strain.

🍽 Add the chestnut paste to 4 litres of stock and simmer for 10 minutes.

🍽 Season with salt and pepper and serve with freshly grated parmesan and fresh bread.

Serves 6-8

Roast quail with chestnuts and cabbage

Chestnut meringue cakes

INGREDIENTS

20g butter

120g icing sugar

2 egg whites

800g chestnuts

2 tbsp caster sugar

2 tbsp unsweetened cocoa

2 tbsp grand marnier

200g fresh cream

METHOD

🍴 This recipe is from Carla Geri Camporesi's book *Tempo di Castagne* (Chestnut Time).

🍴 Preheat the oven to 100C and butter a baking sheet. Add the icing sugar to the eggs and whisk until stiff. Using an icing bag with a scalloped nozzle, pipe 20 little meringues, about the size of a small walnut, onto the buttered baking sheet. Put this into the oven and immediately turn off the heat, leaving the meringues inside for about an hour.

🍴 Meanwhile boil the chestnuts, peel them and remove the inside skins. Rub them through a sieve into a bowl; add caster sugar, the cocoa and the grand marnier and blend everything together. Finally, stir in 80ml of the cream and put the bowl in the fridge. Take the meringues out of the oven and detach them from the tray carefully and put them on a smooth surface to dry. Whip the rest of the cream till reasonably stiff. Spread the whipped cream on each meringue and place neatly onto a serving plate. Using a potato ricer (looks like a big garlic press) cover each meringue with the chestnut mixture. The mixture should fall on the meringues in long, worm-like strands.

🍴 Keep in the fridge until ready to serve.

Serves 4-5

INGREDIENTS

500g fresh chestnuts

4 tbsp extra virgin olive oil

1 onion, chopped

2-3 garlic cloves, sliced

¼ cabbage head, sliced

3 tomatoes, chopped

handful chopped parsley

1 tbsp fresh thyme

salt and pepper

METHOD

🍴 Roast and peel fresh chestnuts (see method in introduction). In a pan heat extra virgin olive oil and lightly fry chopped onion, sliced garlic cloves, sliced cabbage and the chestnuts for 7-8 minutes until the cabbage softens. Add tomatoes and simmer a further 5 minutes. Add chopped parsley, fresh thyme and season with salt and pepper. Serve with roast quail, roast duck or roast chicken.

Serves 8

FIELD MUSHROOMS

Autumn brings a profusion of mushroom species into our markets. While the wild foraged pine mushrooms – the slippery jack and saffron milk cap – bring the humus and resin-scented woods to our tables, there is an increase in the cultivated species.

The ordinary cultivated mushroom (*Agaricus bisporus*), most often seen as small buttons and larger open caps, seems to react to the season by growing to full maturity. At this time of year, field and cultivated mushrooms are larger, meatier and tastier.

A close relative, the Swiss brown, is another of the cultivated species that bulks up in autumn. When it opens fully, sometimes to the size of a small plate, it's known as a portobello, giant cremini or Roman brown mushroom. Their large size, rich flavour and meaty texture are ideally suited to grilling or roasting.

Stuffed large mushrooms are easy to prepare and a good way to use up leftover risotto and couscous. When roasted, the risotto tends to form a crisp crust, while the meaty mushroom remains soft and juicy. The only mushrooms I peel are the wild slippery jacks. I also remove the soggy sponge below the cap leaving only the bright yellow flesh. For other varieties, I find it adequate to use a soft brush to remove any dirt.

Field mushrooms go with
Butter; extra virgin olive oil; onions; leeks; garlic; herbs such as chives, parsley, coriander, thyme and oregano; cheeses, including parmesan, pecorino and goat's; rice; pasta; couscous; polenta; beef; chicken; veal; potatoes; spinach; eggs; lemon; toast; breadcrumbs; vinegar; pepper; chilli; red and white wine.

Field mushroom sauce

INGREDIENTS
6 tbsp extra virgin olive oil
1 medium-sized onion, chopped
2 garlic cloves, minced
6 anchovies
200g field mushrooms, sliced
200g ripe tomatoes, chopped
½ cup chopped parsley
salt and pepper

METHOD
- In a pan heat extra virgin olive oil and fry chopped onion, minced garlic and anchovies for 2 minutes. Add sliced field mushrooms and keep cooking for 3-4 minutes more, constantly stirring. Add chopped, ripe tomatoes and simmer slowly for 20 minutes.
- To finish, add chopped parsley and season with salt and pepper to taste.
- Serve as an accompaniment to grilled meat, as a relish on sandwiches or as a pasta sauce.

Serves 4

Potatoes, field mushrooms and sage

INGREDIENTS
200g firm field mushrooms
600g waxy potatoes
100g butter
4 tbsp extra virgin olive oil
½ cup fresh sage leaves
salt and pepper

METHOD
- Cut the mushrooms into 5mm-thick slices. Peel the potatoes and boil them in plenty of salted water till tender. Cut them into slices of similar size to the mushrooms. Heat half the butter and oil in a pan and fry the mushrooms till golden. Remove the cooked mushrooms from the pan and place on a warm plate.
- Heat the rest of the butter and oil in the pan on a moderate flame. Add the sliced potatoes and the sage and fry till the potatoes are brown and the sage crisp. Add back in the mushrooms and fry for 1-2 minutes.
- Season with salt and pepper.

Serves 4

Whole roasted field mushrooms

INGREDIENTS

large field mushrooms (one per person)

1 cup extra virgin olive oil

5 garlic cloves, peeled and chopped,

½ cup roughly chopped parsley

handful chopped coriander

handful chopped chives

salt and pepper

METHOD

- Allow one large field mushroom per person. Make sure the gills are showing and any dirt on the cap has been brushed off. Cut the woody end of the stalk off and lay the mushrooms, bottoms up, in a baking tray.
- In a bowl, mix extra virgin olive oil with chopped garlic, roughly chopped parsley, coriander and chives. Mix thoroughly and distribute two spoonfuls evenly over the gills of each mushroom.
- With the dressing left, paint the edges and sides of the fungi. Season well with salt and freshly grated pepper. Roast in a preheated 180C oven for 15-20 minutes, depending on their size.
- Before serving, squeeze a little lemon juice on each.

Makes dressing for 10-12

FIGS

My favourite way of eating figs is straight off the tree. But they have to be perfectly ripe. Shop-bought figs are generally too firm so you have to hunt around for fruiterers who know about figs. Once they're picked, they won't ripen any further.

If all you can find are firm figs, then poaching or baking them in liquid will add flavour and soften them up. A good sweet wine and the addition of sugar or honey will improve them. Plain water instead of wine will do but, in that case, more sugar needs to be added. After the figs have been cooked, the remaining liquid can be reduced to a rich syrupy sauce as an accompaniment to the poached fruit.

Figs don't always have to live at the sweet end of the meal. Poached in stock, then dressed with good olive oil and vinegar, they're perfect with rich meat such as grilled or roast quail, kangaroo or venison.

But if you intend to caramelise figs (halve them, sugar the cut surfaces and blowtorch them till golden), serve them with prosciutto or jamon, or bake them quickly with gorgonzola, then they have to be perfectly soft and ripe.

Roast pigeon and fig salad

INGREDIENTS

plump pigeons (one per person)
olive oil
salt and pepper
handful bitter lettuce (endive, radicchio or rocket)
2 ripe figs, sliced into wedges
balsamic vinegar

METHOD

🍽 Allow one plump pigeon between two people. If unavailable, a quail each will work well. Preheat the oven to 240C. Rub the pigeon with olive oil, salt and pepper and roast for 10-12 minutes. Leave it in its pan to rest.

🍽 Take a good handful of your favourite bitter lettuce – endive, radicchio or rocket. Place in a bowl with two ripe figs sliced into wedges. Cut the pigeon breasts off the bone and slice into bite-sized pieces. Cut the legs into thigh and drumstick and add to the salad.

🍽 Dress with a little olive oil and balsamic vinegar. Season, toss and serve.

Serves 1

Figs with stracchino and honey

INGREDIENTS

1 tbsp light-coloured honey – acacia, citrus blossom, clover or similar
3 tbsp extra virgin olive oil
1 tbsp red wine vinegar
700g ripe figs, green or black
250g soft stracchino cheese, goat's curd, or young pecorino
1 good-sized bunch of large rocket leaves, washed and cut
¼ cup fresh basil leaves
salt and freshly ground pepper

METHOD

🍽 Mix together the honey, olive oil and vinegar until homogenous. Cut the figs into wedges. Tear the stracchino into bite-sized pieces. Toss all the ingredients together carefully with the dressing. Season with salt and freshly ground black pepper and serve.

Serves 4

Figs go with

Salt-cured and air-dried ham such as prosciutto and Spanish ham; soft cheeses such as gorgonzola, brie and goat's curd; nuts; orange and lemon; honey; sugar; rocket, radicchio and fennel; roast pigeon, grilled quail and roast duck; mascarpone; cream; butter; balsamic vinegar; vincotto; brandy, cognac and armagnac.

Caramelised figs with cream and vincotto

INGREDIENTS

figs (one per person)

caster sugar

whipped or double cream

vincotto or good balsamic vinegar

METHOD

Allow one large fig or two small ones per person. Cut the figs in half, top to bottom, and lay them cut-side up on a heatproof tray. Sprinkle a teaspoon of caster sugar on each half fig. Caramelise the sugar using a blowtorch or, if you prefer, place the tray under a grill on medium heat. When the sugar has turned a golden caramel colour, the figs are ready. To serve, place a dollop or two of whipped or double cream on a plate.

Place the fig halves on the cream and drizzle a little vincotto over the lot. If unavailable, a few drops of good balsamic vinegar will do. (Vincotto, also called saba, is an Italian sweet condiment made from boiled grape must.)

Serves 1

LENTILS

As the days cool a little, appetites grow keener for foods that give warmth and comfort. The cook senses this change and thoughts turn to ingredients that require slower cooking. To my mind, lentils are the perfect comfort food – soothing, flavoursome and able to absorb many other flavours.

To prepare, they need to be meticulously sorted to make sure there are no small stones hiding among them. The stones have a way of looking just like lentils but of course, once cooked, do not soften; so a little time should be put aside initially so that nobody chips a tooth.

Unlike other dried pulses, such as beans and chickpeas, lentils need not be soaked overnight before cooking. They should be washed well to rid them of dust and dirt only. Cooked lentils soak up enormous quantities of liquid in proportion to their size so, if they end up being a little dry, add some hot broth or water to moisten them before serving.

As a general rule, lentils, once cooked, will swell to about twice their volume.

Lentil soup with pork sausages

INGREDIENTS
400g lentils
3 garlic cloves, peeled and chopped
1 chopped onion
1 bay leaf
150g pureed ripe tomatoes
500g good quality pork sausages
salt and pepper

METHOD
- Wash lentils well. Drain, transfer them to a pot, and cover with lightly salted cold water. Bring the pot to a simmer, add garlic, onion, bay leaf and tomatoes. Cover and simmer gently for about 90 minutes. While the lentils are cooking, bring a pot of water to a simmer and place in whole, good quality pork sausages. Simmer for 3-5 minutes, remove from the water and cool for a couple of minutes.
- When the soup is ready, season with salt and pepper. Add the sausages, cut into small chunks, and serve with a drizzle of extra virgin olive oil.

Serves 8

Lentils go with
Extra virgin olive oil; butter; onion; garlic; carrot; celery; tomato; spinach; herbs such as sage, parsley, thyme and coriander; bay leaf; saffron; lamb; beef; venison; quails; pigeon; stuffed pig's trotter; poached veal and ox tongue; pork belly; sausages; cotechino; ham; all flatbreads.

Lamb and lentil tagine

INGREDIENTS

1/3 cup extra virgin olive oil

pinch saffron

1 tsp powdered turmeric

1 tbsp grated fresh ginger

1 onion, chopped

2 carrots, chopped

1 celery heart, chopped

1 cup lentils

1 lamb shoulder, cut into 2cm
    pieces

salt and pepper

1 bunch coriander, chopped

juice of 1 lemon

METHOD

🍽 Gently heat extra virgin olive oil in a tagine base or heavy casserole pot, and add saffron, powdered turmeric and grated fresh ginger. Lightly fry for a minute then add chopped onion, carrots and celery heart (including the tender celery leaves). Stir well and lightly fry for 2-3 minutes. Add well-washed lentils and lamb shoulder pieces. Mix well and add enough water to just cover all the ingredients. Season with salt and pepper, stir, and place the lid on. Place the tagine (or casserole) into a preheated 180C oven for 50-70 minutes until the lamb and lentils are thoroughly cooked.

🍽 Once out of the oven, roughly chop a bunch of coriander and squeeze in the juice of a lemon. Check for seasoning and serve.

Serves 6

Lentil puree with crostini

INGREDIENTS

500g lentils

1 stick celery, washed and cut into 1cm rounds

1 carrot, peeled and cut into 1cm rounds

1 onion, peeled and sliced

1 potato, peeled and chopped into 2cm dice

1 ripe tomato, washed and roughly chopped

¼ cup parsley

80g grated parmesan

6 tbsp extra virgin olive oil

6 slices of day-old bread

salt and pepper

METHOD

🍽 Cook the lentils by washing them well first and placing in a pot covered with water. Bring to the boil, turn down to a simmer and cook, covered, for 30 minutes or more (depending on the lentil) till tender. Place the celery, carrot, potato, onion and tomato in a pot and cover with water. Bring to the boil and turn down to a simmer. Keep simmering until the vegetables are soft.

🍽 Add the drained lentils and parsley to the vegetables and bring back to the boil. Turn down to a simmer and keep simmering for 10 minutes. Put the contents through a mouli or food processor and puree. Add the parmesan and season with salt and pepper. Place 4 tablespoons of the olive oil in a pan and fry the slices of bread on both sides till golden.

🍽 Serve the puree on the crostini with a drizzle of the remaining oil.

Serves 6

MANDARINS

The scent of mandarin is one of the most evocative and memorable of all. As kids, we used to take freshly peeled skin and squeeze it so its pungent oils would spurt into each other's eyes.

The effect of stinging – momentary blindness coupled with that particularly sweet smell – is a memory that returns for me year after year with the first fruit of the season.

One of the most delicious mandarin desserts I have tasted was a warm, sweet, bean soup in a Chinese restaurant in Hong Kong. The beans were flavoured with highly perfumed dried mandarin peel. Just a couple of pieces were enough to convert simple beans into a memorable dish.

The mandarin most widely available is the imperial, which has smooth skin and sweet, juicy flesh. Another tasty variety early in the season is the page, although it looks more like an orange than a mandarin.

Look out for the early to mid-season fremont variety – a little harder to peel but often with a more concentrated flavour. Late in winter and well into spring, the honey murcott mandarin ripens. It is unsurpassed for the sweetness and flavour of its juice.

What to look for
Fruit that feels heavy with juice and has glossy skin. While some varieties have naturally loose skin, avoid fruit that looks puffy and smells overripe.

Mandarins go with
Cream; yoghurt; custard; sugar; honey; lime and lemon; vanilla; cinnamon and cassia; coconut milk; black sticky rice; chocolate; fennel; crab; prawns; lobster; roast duck; roast quail; rum; brandy, especially cognac and armagnac; grappa; sponge cake; strawberries, raspberries and blueberries.

Sliced mandarins with honey and lavender

INGREDIENTS
1/3 cup mild-tasting honey
1 tsp dried lavender
450g mandarins

METHOD
- This is a dish from *Chez Panisse Fruit* by Alice Waters.
- Heat mild-tasting honey such as clover or orange blossom over low heat. Crush dried lavender and mix it with the honey, letting it steep for 30 to 40 minutes. Strain the honey.
- Peel mandarins and, keeping them whole, cut horizontal slices 1cm thick and lay them side by side on serving plates. Finish by drizzling them with the lavender-flavoured honey.

Serves 4

Mandarin and raisin compote

INGREDIENTS
180ml mandarin juice
4 pieces of mandarin rind, peeled off using a potato peeler
1 cup seedless raisins
65g sugar
60ml OP rum
2 tbsp unsalted butter, softened

METHOD
- Place the juice, rind, raisins, sugar and rum in a saucepan and simmer until the raisins are plump. Strain the liquid and keep the raisins and peel in a bowl. Return the liquid to the saucepan and reduce over a moderate heat until it is syrupy (about half a cup).
- Take the pan from the heat and whisk in the butter. Pour the sauce over the raisins and peel, mix together and cool to room temperature.
- Use as an accompaniment to panna cotta, gelato, tea cakes and biscotti.

Makes about 425ml compote

Crab, mandarin and fennel salad

INGREDIENTS

2 medium-sized fennel bulbs

3-4 tbsp extra virgin olive oil

2 tbsp red wine vinegar

salt and pepper

2 mandarins

320g cooked crabmeat

METHOD

- Peel the tough outer layers of the fennel bulbs, keeping some of the feathery green tops. Thinly slice the fennel hearts and toss them with extra virgin olive oil and red wine vinegar. Season with salt and pepper and lay the fennel on one large or four smaller plates, keeping the remaining dressing.

- Peel mandarins and remove the hairy pith. Separate the segments, slice each in half lengthways and remove any seeds. Scatter the segments on top of the fennel. Pick through cooked crabmeat, making sure there is no shell among the meat. Scatter the crab neatly on the salad and drizzle the rest of the dressing on it. Finish by chopping the fennel tops and add them as a final green flourish.

Serves 4

FENNEL

If you look carefully at the fennel displayed in the shops you'll see that there are two distinct shapes. One is more squat and bulbous and the other is thinner, more elongated and taller. And as far as taste and texture go, they are very different.

The fatter bulb is tenderer and has a delicate flavour. This is the one that is more suited to eating raw in salads or simply cut into wedges and dipped into good extra virgin olive oil. The more elongated one is stringier, a little tougher in texture and has a more pronounced aniseed-like flavour. For braised or slow-cooked dishes the latter fares better.

You'll also notice that, as the weather gets colder, fennel gets bigger and fatter. It loves the cold. Sure, fennel is around in summer but the bulbs are small and wiry and lack the crisp texture of winter bulbs.

For something a little different, dice some fennel, along with other vegetables for a hearty winter soup. Keep those wispy fronds to add, chopped, as a last minute addition with the grated parmesan.

Fennel's flavour marries well with a seafood stew. Simmer some chopped onion, garlic and fennel in some olive oil till soft. Add a teaspoon of fennel seed for added flavour then pour in a litre of water and a cup of tomato puree. Bring to the boil, season with salt and then add your favourite seafood till just cooked.

Fried fennel

INGREDIENTS
4 medium-sized fennel bulbs, tough outer layers removed
2 eggs
150ml extra virgin olive oil
3 tbsp plain flour
salt

METHOD
After having removed the tough outer layers from each fennel bulb, cut each into six wedges. Bring a pot of salted water to the boil and blanch the fennel for 4-6 minutes till tender. Remove from the water, set onto a clean towel and pat dry. Beat the eggs lightly in a bowl. Heat the olive oil in a frypan. Dip each fennel wedge into the egg, dust with the flour and fry till golden on each side. Place on some absorbent paper to drain. Season with salt and serve.

Serves 4

Roast fennel

INGREDIENTS
2 large fennel bulbs
100g parmesan, finely grated
3 tbsp extra virgin olive oil
salt and pepper

METHOD
Trim the fennel bulbs and cut each into six wedges. Cook the fennel by simmering in water until each wedge has softened (about 2-3 minutes), though it should still be a little firm. Do not overcook. Drain and cool. Fill the folds of the fennel wedges with the grated parmesan, season each with salt and pepper and place on a roasting tray that has been brushed with olive oil. Sprinkle the olive oil on the fennel and roast in a preheated oven at 180C until the faces of the fennel quarters are golden. This should take 7-8 minutes.

Serves 4 as a side

Fennel goes with
Extra virgin olive oil; sesame oil; butter; parmesan; aged goat's milk and sheep's milk cheeses; oranges, especially navels and blood; lemon juice; vinegars; olives; walnuts; hazelnuts; tomatoes; asparagus; green beans; garlic; poultry, especially chicken, pheasant and duck; rabbit; eggs; cream; salad leaves, especially rocket, radicchio and watercress; fish; good sea salt and freshly cracked pepper; anchovies; capers; parsley and coriander.

Fennel with capers and anchovies

INGREDIENTS

2 large fennel bulbs, with their green tops intact

4 tbsp extra virgin olive oil

3 anchovies

1 handful breadcrumbs, not too fine

½ tbsp capers, rinsed well and patted dry

¼ cup young flat-leaf parsley leaves

30g pecorino or parmesan cheese, shaved

salt and pepper

METHOD

🍽 Trim the fennel bulbs by discarding their tough, external layers. Keep the tender fronds from the heads and soak in cold water. Wash the bulbs well and cut into thin slices top to bottom. Bring a saucepan of salted water to the boil and plunge in the fennel slices. Blanch for 2 minutes till tender, drain and set aside to cool.

🍽 Meanwhile, heat the olive oil gently in a saucepan and add the anchovies, stirring until they have dissolved. Add the breadcrumbs and a pinch of freshly cracked pepper. Stir for a minute, add the drained fennel slices and mix well. Take from the heat and add the capers, parsley, fennel tops and cheese. Season with salt and pepper to taste, mix well and transfer to a serving plate.

Serves 4

PERSIMMONS

When the luscious, messily delicious fruits of summer have all but gone and autumn rolls on, the persimmon ripens to a soft, gooey jam the colour of burnt orange and its skin thins until it finally cracks like that of fig. For these reasons, the persimmon is not a very co-operative commercial fruit, but is worth seeking out for its outstanding flavour and texture.

The tree, however, is often planted in gardens for its ornamental qualities and even after it drops its leaves in late autumn or early winter, the bright orange fruit clings to the bare branches.

Of the fruit, there are two distinct types. The non-astringent variety, which is flat and almost boxy in shape, can be eaten while it is still as crisp as an apple. The astringent type, however, which looks more like an acorn-shaped tomato, contains tannic acid, and must ripen fully, until the flesh is jelly-like and very sweet, before it can be eaten.

To ripen persimmons, place them on a tray or a plate out of the refrigerator until very soft. The ripening time will depend on their maturity when picked. Persimmon is one of my favourite fruits for breakfast – halved and the flesh spooned out and eaten, or smothered like jam on toast.

Persimmon biscuits

INGREDIENTS

125g butter
250g sugar
1 cup ripe persimmon pulp
1 egg
2¼ cups plain flour
1 tsp baking powder
1 cup chopped roasted
  hazelnuts
1 cup sultanas
½ tsp ground cinnamon
½ tsp ground cloves
½ tsp ground nutmeg

METHOD

◉ Cream butter and sugar. Mix in ripe persimmon pulp and whole egg. Sift plain flour and baking powder together and mix in. Add chopped, roasted hazelnuts, sultanas and ground cinnamon, ground cloves and ground nutmeg. Drop with a teaspoon onto greased baking trays. Bake for 10 minutes in a preheated 190C oven.

Makes about 90 biscuits

Persimmons go with
Cream; icecream; custard; yoghurt; sugar; honey; palm sugar; bread; sponge cake; bread-and-butter pudding; pannacotta; creme brulee; vanilla; cloves; nutmeg; star anise; cinnamon; ginger; aniseed; nuts including pinenuts, walnuts, hazelnuts and almonds; lime and lemon juice; raisins; sultanas.

Persimmon and pinenut bread

Persimmon and chocolate torta

INGREDIENTS

4 eggs, separated

130g caster sugar

150g milk chocolate

50g rum

100g savoiardi (Italian biscuits)

2 large persimmons, soft and ripe

juice of 1 lemon

1 large persimmon for decoration

METHOD

🍽 Beat the egg yolks with 100g of the caster sugar till pale and smooth. Melt the chocolate carefully in a double boiler and mix with the egg yolk and sugar mixture. Stir in half the rum. Beat the egg whites till they form firm peaks. Fold these into the chocolate mixture.

🍽 Line a 22cm-torte tin (with a removable base) with silicone paper on both base and sides. Arrange the savoiardi on the base, cut to fit if necessary. Pour the chocolate mixture on top of the biscuits and freeze for 3-4 hours.

🍽 Meanwhile, peel and seed the two persimmons and puree the flesh till smooth. In a saucepan, place the remaining sugar and rum, the lemon juice and half the persimmon puree (refrigerate the remaining half). Bring the saucepan's contents to the boil and simmer for 5 minutes. Cool completely and add the refrigerated persimmon puree.

🍽 To serve, remove the torte from the tin and peel off the silicone paper carefully from the sides (leave the bottom ring on). Slice the remaining persimmon and decorate the top. Serve with the persimmon sauce.

Serves 8-10

INGREDIENTS

185g unsalted butter

1 cup sugar

2 eggs, beaten

2 cups plain four

1 tsp bicarb soda

400ml ripe persimmon pulp

½ cup pinenuts

METHOD

🍽 Cream unsalted butter with sugar. Add beaten eggs and mix. Sift plain flour and bicarb soda together and mix in. Add soft, ripe persimmon pulp and pinenuts and mix – the dough should be quite firm. Butter and flour two 26cm-long by 10cm-wide loaf tins and distribute the dough evenly. Place into a preheated 170C oven for an hour. Cool before slicing. To serve, whip some single cream with a little vanilla.

🍽 Cut the persimmon and pinenut bread into 1cm-thick slices (toast them if you like). Top with the cream and half a ripe persimmon.

Serves 10

POLENTA

Even before the introduction of corn in the 16th century, polenta had been the staple of the poor in northern Italy for hundreds of years.

Before then, it consisted of grains and legumes mashed and cooked to a gruel-like mush. Once corn was introduced, farmers found that it produced more than other grains on the limited land area. Eventually it became synonymous with polenta.

There's a great scene in Bernardo Bertolucci's film *1900* where the labourers are seated along a huge table for lunch. Two women turn out a steaming cauldron of polenta onto a large wooden board. It flows out like golden lava and then sets before reaching the edges of the board. While still hot, the women slip a length of string between polenta and board, dividing the cake into wedges.

These days, polenta is a fashionable ingredient and still very simple and inexpensive to make. The main thing is to avoid lumps by slowly adding the corn meal to boiling water while stirring. If spooning from the pot, always dip the spoon in water beforehand; the polenta is less likely to stick.

Polenta goes with

Butter; milk; cream; cheeses, especially parmesan, taleggio, fontina and gruyere; mushrooms; ossobuco; braised lamb shanks; fried prosciutto; sausages; pig's trotters; pork belly; chicken and duck livers; sweet and sour cabbage; tomato salsa; roast garlic; grilled scallops; herbs such as sage, rosemary and parsley.

Polenta fritters

INGREDIENTS

polenta
slices of prosciutto
slices of fontina or gruyere
egg
grated parmesan
breadcrumbs
olive oil

METHOD

◉ This is a good dish for leftover polenta. "Set" the polenta in a tray to about 5mm thickness and refrigerate. Cut into 5cm squares or discs. Place a thin slice of prosciutto and one of fontina or gruyere between two pieces of polenta. Dip the fritters in egg wash, dredge in a mixture of one-third grated parmesan and two-thirds breadcrumbs and shallow fry them till golden in olive oil or butter.

Serves 1

Torta sbrisolona

INGREDIENTS

125g plain flour
80g fine polenta
100g blanched almond meal
80g caster sugar
1 egg yolk
juice of ½ lemon
rind of 1 lemon, grated
60g butter
50g duck or goose fat (or extra virgin olive oil)

METHOD

◉ This polenta shortbread is a feature of Lombard cuisine and is sold in most cake shops where this tradition is practised.

◉ Mix the flour and polenta with the almond meal, sugar, egg yolk, lemon juice and rind. Incorporate the butter and the duck fat. Press into a buttered baking tray to a thickness of 2cm and bake for 30 minutes at 170C. Cool before serving.

Serves 6-8

Polenta with mushrooms

INGREDIENTS

5 cups water

½ tsp salt

1 cup polenta flour

1 tbsp butter

1 tbsp extra virgin olive oil

1 medium-sized onion, chopped

6 garlic cloves, minced

500g mushrooms (mix of wild and cultivated plus a few dried porcini), sliced

handful chopped parsley

salt and pepper

2 knobs butter

METHOD

Bring water to the boil. Add salt, then slowly add polenta flour, stirring constantly with a wooden spoon or a whisk until the polenta comes away from the sides of the saucepan. Turn heat down very low to a simmer and place a lid on. Simmer for about 20-30 minutes, giving it a good stir every 5 minutes. The polenta should be soft and tender, but not runny. The longer it's cooked, the thicker and more flavoursome it will be.

Meanwhile, heat butter and extra virgin olive oil in a pan and gently fry chopped onion and minced cloves of garlic for 30 seconds. Add sliced mushrooms (make this a mixture of wild and cultivated as well as a few dried porcini) and stir continuously at a high heat until they soften – about 2-3 minutes. Lower the heat and simmer for about 15 minutes. Add chopped parsley, season with salt and pepper and stir in another couple of knobs of butter.

Serve on top of the polenta with plenty of freshly grated parmesan.

Makes sauce for 6

PORCINI

Make the most of the rich flavour and meaty texture of porcini mushrooms.

Porcini are among the most flavoursome and sought-after mushrooms in the world. They are gathered wild in European forests but grow in North America, China and South Africa as well. Anyone who has been in Italy during autumn and tasted fresh porcini grilled over coals with olive oil, parsley and garlic will never forget that incomparable flavour and meaty texture.

Growing wild, with glossy brown caps like glazed buns and bulging, belly-like stems, these mushrooms look like piglets, hence their name.

When sliced and dried slowly, porcini seem to concentrate their flavour and aroma. Dried porcini are perhaps not as indispensable as parmesan or extra virgin olive oil, but are essential when I want to add an earthy mushroom boost to a dish where bland cultivated mushrooms are used. A classic mushroom risotto needs only a few dried porcini slices, some good stock, Italian rice, butter and parmesan. Add some to a minestrone or chicken soup; chop some into a stuffing for quail, chicken or even meatloaf.

New-season porcini, mostly imported from Italy and France, are being picked and dried now. There are some frozen whole porcini available, but I have always found these disappointing. Good dried porcini will have a powerful aroma. Avoid powder or tiny pieces, which are usually produced from secondary grades.

Rigatoni with lentils and porcini

INGREDIENTS

handful dried porcini (about 50g)

2 cups cold water

2 celery sticks

3 garlic cloves, peeled

1 small onion

1 carrot

3 tbsp extra virgin olive oil

2 cups lentils, washed

2 ripe tomatoes, chopped

salt and pepper

500g rigatoni

handful chopped parsley

METHOD

- Soak dried porcini in cold water. Before using, drain well and squeeze. Finely chop sticks of celery, cloves of garlic, small onion and carrot. Heat extra virgin olive oil in a saucepan and fry the vegetables for 2 minutes until soft. Add washed lentils and chopped ripe tomatoes and cover with water. Simmer until the lentils are cooked (about 25-35 minutes), season with salt and pepper.
- Cook 500g of rigatoni and drain well. Toss the lentils with the pasta, drizzle on a little olive oil and add a handful of chopped parsley.
- Serve with grated pecorino or parmesan.

Serves 4

Porcini go with

Butter and extra virgin olive oil; parmesan, pecorino and goat's cheese; rice; pasta; couscous; polenta; beef; veal; chicken; game meats such as hare, duck, quail, pigeon, rabbit and venison; potatoes; eggs; onions; garlic; spring onions; leeks; bread; vinegar; parsley; coriander; thyme; pepper; chilli; red and white wine.

Porcini on toast

Porcini and celeriac puree

INGREDIENTS

500g celeriac, peeled cut into quarters

100g butter

1 garlic clove, roasted whole

2 tbsp extra virgin olive oil

1 onion, peeled and finely diced

30g dried porcini, reconstituted in cold water for 10 minutes

salt and pepper

METHOD

Cook the celeriac by simmering in water until the pieces have softened. Do not overcook. Drain and place in a food processor with the butter and seasoning, and puree. Check for seasoning and adjust. The garlic should be roasted until the cloves have lost their firmness but have not turned to a puree. Peel the cloves, cut each into three chunks and mix them through the celeriac puree. This is easier when the puree is still warm.

Heat the olive oil in a pan and fry the onion gently till it is transparent. Drain the porcini, pat dry and chop. Add to the onion and lightly fry for a minute. Mix the onion and porcini in the celeriac puree.

Makes a great accompaniment to roast duck, quail or other rich game meats.

Serves 8

INGREDIENTS

handful dried porcini

2 cups cold water

300-400g mixed fresh mushrooms

3-4 tbsp extra virgin olive oil

1 onion, finely chopped

3 garlic cloves, minced

½ cup roughly chopped flat-leaf parsley

salt and pepper

METHOD

Soak dried porcini (about 50g) in cold water until soft – about 5 minutes. Before using, drain well and squeeze. Cut mixture of fresh mushrooms into thin slices.

Heat extra virgin olive oil in a pan and gently fry finely chopped onion and minced garlic cloves for 30 seconds. Add the mushrooms and stir until they wilt – about 3 minutes. Add roughly chopped flat-leaf parsley, season with salt and pepper and stir. Cook for 5 minutes and serve on toast.

Serves 8

SUGAR PLUMS

Any mention of the sugar plum is most likely going to make you think of Tchaikovsky's *Nutcracker Suite*, fairies, sugar-coated sweets or even Eugene Field's poem about the sugar plum tree that "blooms on the shore of the Lollipop sea/In the garden of Shut-Eye Town".

But the sugar plum is also a real fruit. It's a small- to medium-sized, grape-shaped plum with red to dark-red skin and sweet yellow-green flesh. As a stone fruit it's a late arrival but, because it takes its time to ripen, the sugar plum is one of the sweetest of all the prunus family.

Unlike many other plums, its skin is not astringent; it is thin and breaks down easily once cooked, making the sugar plum ideal for compotes and jams. Bubbled in a pot for 10 minutes or so with tangy rhubarb and a little sugar, it makes a wonderful filling for pancakes, scones or a sponge cake.

Sugar plums go with
Sugar; honey; cinnamon; cardamom; nutmeg; almonds; hazelnuts; peaches; apricots; nectarines; rhubarb; orange and lemon zest; dates; dried fruits; sweet pastry, especially puff and shortcrust; sweet pizza; toast; scones; pancakes and pikelets; pork; rabbit; yoghurt; cream; icecream; mascarpone; clotted cream.

Sugar plum upside-down tart

INGREDIENTS

sheet of puff pastry
250ml water
150g caster sugar, plus extra
75g unsalted butter
350g pitted and halved sugar plums

METHOD

- Roll out a circle of puff pastry dough a little bigger than a 28cm pie tin. Make sure the pastry is rolled thin, then chill in the refrigerator. Heat water and caster sugar in a frypan until the mixture bubbles. Keep cooking until it is a light golden caramel colour then add unsalted butter. Keep it bubbling, without stirring, for a minute and then add pitted and halved sugar plums. Cook the side of each plum for 2 minutes then place them, skin-side down in an even layer, in the pie tin. Pour in the caramel butter, making sure it does not reach the top. Place the chilled pastry disc on top and sprinkle a little caster sugar on top. Put the pie tin on a tray and bake in a preheated 190C oven for 25-30 minutes until the pastry is cooked.
- Remove and carefully turn upside down on a serving plate so that the fruit is on top. Serve hot or cold with cream or icecream.

Serves 8

Sugar plum crumble

INGREDIENTS

150g plain flour

50g almond meal

100g sugar

50g dark brown sugar

½ tsp ground cinnamon

½ tsp ground cardamom

120g butter, melted

1kg sugar plums

50g sugar

METHOD

🍴 Preheat the oven to 190C. In a bowl, whisk together plain flour, almond meal, 100g sugar, 50g dark brown sugar, ground cinnamon and ground cardamom. Slowly drizzle in melted butter and mix with a fork until it forms small crumbs. Break up any large crumbs so that none is bigger than 1cm.

🍴 Pit and quarter sugar plums and toss in a bowl with 50g of sugar. Spoon the plums into buttered individual ovenproof moulds and sprinkle the crumbs evenly on top. Bake for 30 minutes until the fruit is bubbling and the crumble is crisp.

Serves 6-8

Sugar plums with plum brandy mascarpone cream

INGREDIENTS

500g sugar plums, halved and stones removed

125g sugar

½ vanilla bean, split

juice of ½ lemon

small cinnamon stick

125ml double cream

70g caster sugar

250g mascarpone

2 tbsp plum brandy (slivovitz)

METHOD

🍴 Place the sugar plums, 125g sugar, vanilla bean and cinnamon stick in a pan and turn on to a moderate heat. Stir until the plums have softened but not fallen apart. Remove from the pan and cool down to room temperature.

🍴 Meanwhile, beat the double cream with 70g of sugar till firm peaks form. Add the mascarpone and plum brandy and fold in.

🍴 Serve the plums with the cream.

Serves 4-6

SALT COD

The French call it morue, the Spaniards know it as bacalao and in Italy it is baccala. In English it is simply called salt cod. The name refers to a large number of species of the cod family that are salted and air-dried to preserve the flesh.

Salt cod has been an important source of protein in Mediterranean countries since the Middle Ages, though the cod was imported from Scandinavia. In times before refrigeration, the dried cod could be transported, stored and rehydrated when needed.

Over the centuries, thousands of dishes have been devised around this cured fish.

Salt cod goes with

Butter; cream; extra virgin olive oil; potato; onion; garlic; shallots; spring onions; leeks; cabbage; tomato; celery; carrot; peas; chilli and capsicum; herbs such as parsley, tarragon, thyme, oregano and chervil; breadcrumbs; mayonnaise; lemon; polenta; chickpeas; eggs; capers; mustard; anchovies.

Tagliatelle with salt cod sauce and chickpeas

INGREDIENTS

700g piece of salt cod
4 tbsp extra virgin olive oil
3 garlic cloves, minced
1 cup roughly chopped parsley
700g tomatoes, peeled, seeded and chopped
300g cooked chickpeas
salt and pepper
750g tagliatelle

METHOD

- This recipe is adapted from the book *La Cucina Pugliese* by Luigi Sada.
- Soak salt cod (see next recipe for method). Cut into six equal chunks. Heat extra virgin olive oil in a casserole dish and lightly fry minced garlic cloves with roughly chopped parsley. When the cloves turn straw yellow, add peeled, seeded and chopped tomatoes and the fish. Simmer for 30-35 minutes until the fish is tender. Remove the salt cod pieces intact and set aside to serve as a second course with a tossed salad. Add cooked chickpeas to the remaining sauce, season with salt and pepper.
- Cook tagliatelle or other wide ribbon pasta, put it in a bowl and toss it with the chickpeas and the sauce.

Serves 8

Cream of salt cod with garlic crostini

INGREDIENTS

750g piece of salt cod
1 carrot, chopped
1 onion, chopped
1 celery stick, chopped
1 onion, sliced
2 garlic cloves, sliced
1 celery heart, chopped
3 tbsp extra virgin olive oil
½ cup white wine
3 medium-sized potatoes,
  peeled and sliced
1 bay leaf
150g butter
salt and pepper

METHOD

🍽 Prepare salt cod by soaking it in cold water for three days, changing the water each day. Drain, remove the dark skin (it should pull off easily) and cut the fish into smaller pieces that will fit into a pot. Cover with water, add a chopped carrot, onion and a celery stick. Bring to the boil, turn down the heat and simmer for 20 minutes until the fish is tender. Drain it, allow it to cool then strip the meat from the bones and set it aside.

🍽 In another pot, lightly fry a sliced onion, sliced garlic cloves and a chopped celery heart for a couple of minutes in extra virgin olive oil. Add white wine and boil until the wine has almost evaporated. Add potatoes and bay leaf, cover with water and simmer until the vegetables are tender. Remove the bay leaf, add the salt cod pieces and butter while still hot and blend (hand blitz or in food processor) until smooth. Season with salt and white pepper.

🍽 Serve hot with garlic crostini (toasts), adding a sprinkle of parsley and a drizzle of extra virgin olive oil.

Serves 10-12

Baccala with grilled country bread

INGREDIENTS

6 thick slices of country bread
200ml extra virgin olive oil
500g onions, peeled and finely diced
300g ripe tomatoes and chopped
1.2kg salt cod, rehydrated and desalted, cut into bite-sized pieces
2 garlic cloves, peeled
½ cup parsley

METHOD

🍽 Brush the bread slices on each side with a little of the olive oil. Heat the remaining oil in a saucepan and lightly fry the onions until transparent. Add the chopped tomatoes and cook for 2-3 minutes till they break down. Add 1½ litres of water and simmer for 30 minutes. Add the pieces of salt cod and cook for a further 20 minutes.

🍽 Finely chop the garlic and parsley and add to the salt cod. Check for seasoning and correct with salt if necessary and a few turns of pepper.

🍽 Grill or toast the slices of bread and serve the salt cod (baccala) on top of the bread.

Serves 6

SLOW COOKING

In slow cooking we want to break down the connective tissue in meat and turn the collagen into gelatin, rendering the meat tender. Flavour coaxed from the meat is transferred to the cooking liquid, producing the rich sauces that, along with tender, succulent meat, are the two goals of a slow braise. Here is a quick guide:

1. Choose the right cut. Lean meat will turn dry.
2. First, brown the meat in oil. This will add colour and flavour.
3. Add aromatic vegetables, a little spice and some herbs.
4. Add body either by lightly flouring the meat before browning and/or adding a rich stock as the braising liquid.
5. Always simmer slowly, don't boil.
6. Make the dish the day before; it always tastes better.

Slow cooking is good for
Shanks; brisket; shoulder; oxtail and kangaroo tail; duck, quail and hare legs; pork trotters; pork belly; aromatic vegetables such as carrot, onion, garlic and celery; spices such as clove, ginger, cardamom, bay and pepper; herbs such as parsley, rosemary, sage, coriander and thyme; wine; stock.

Slow-roasted pork shoulder with roasted root vegetables

INGREDIENTS

1 pork shoulder, boned and rolled, skin left on and tied securely
10 tbsp extra virgin olive oil
5 sprigs rosemary
5 sprigs sage
2 carrots, peeled and cut into 2cm cubes
2 parsnips, peeled and cut into 2cm cubes
1 celeriac, peeled and cut into 2cm cubes
20 baby beetroot, trimmed and left whole with skin on
¼ cup chopped parsley
15 garlic cloves, peeled and left whole
salt and pepper

METHOD

- Score the pork skin well with a sharp knife then brush it with 2 tablespoons of the olive oil and generously sprinkle with salt.
- In a large pan heat another 2 tablespoons of olive oil and fry the rolled shoulder, giving the skin some colour.
- In a roasting pan lay the rosemary stalks and sage down with the rolled shoulder on top. Roast in a preheated 160C oven for about 3 hours.
- Meanwhile, place the root vegetables and the garlic in a roasting pan, toss them with the remaining 6 tablespoons of olive oil, salt and pepper and roast at 200C for about 20 minutes, turning them over every few minutes so they become well coloured and golden.
- To serve, slice the shoulder accompanied by the roast root vegetables.

Serves 8

Ossobuco

INGREDIENTS

6 pieces of ossobuco

plain flour, for dusting

olive oil, for frying

3 onions, chopped

salt and pepper

5 ripe tomatoes, pureed

dry white wine

½ cup chopped parsley

5 garlic cloves, minced

METHOD

🍽 Dust pieces of ossobuco (veal shank from the hind leg, cut across the bone, each piece about 4cm thick) with plain flour, heat some olive oil in a skillet and brown the meat lightly.

🍽 In a pot large enough to hold all the ossobuco, sauté chopped onions in a little olive oil, making sure they become transparent but don't colour. Arrange the ossobuco on top of the onions, season a little with salt and pepper, add pureed ripe tomatoes and enough dry white wine so that the meat is almost covered. Bring this to the boil, then lower the heat and simmer, covered, for 90 minutes. After that time, add chopped parsley and minced garlic cloves, and simmer for another 30 minutes.

🍽 Season with salt and pepper and serve by itself or with polenta or saffron risotto.

Serves 6

Braised beef shoulder in shiraz

INGREDIENTS

1.5kg shoulder of beef, tied with butcher's twine

2-3 tbsp extra virgin olive oil

3 onions, peeled and chopped

3 carrots, peeled and chopped

stem of rosemary (5cm long)

3 garlic cloves, peeled

1 celery heart, chopped

2 bay leaves

4 whole cloves

1.5 litres shiraz

2 pinches of salt

freshly ground pepper

METHOD

🍽 Get your butcher to prepare a 1.5kg piece of beef shoulder and ask to have it tied well with butcher's twine. Heat extra virgin olive oil in a braising pan and brown the meat well. Remove the meat from the pan and add chopped onions, chopped carrots, stem of rosemary, whole garlic cloves, chopped celery heart, bay leaves and whole cloves. Lightly fry the vegetables for 2-3 minutes, constantly stirring.

🍽 Place the meat on top of the vegetables and add shiraz. Add a couple of good pinches of salt and some freshly ground pepper. Bring to the boil then reduce the heat to a simmer, cover and cook slowly for at least 2 hours. Once done, strain the vegetables and discard the rosemary, bay leaves and cloves.

🍽 Puree the vegetables through a fine sieve or in a food processor. Return the puree to the braising liquid and adjust the seasoning.

🍽 Serve the shoulder sliced with the sauce.

Serves 6

SALT

Salt is the taste on your skin as it dries after a swim in the surf. Sometimes, if you've spent the entire day in and out of the ocean, there's so much salt on your body that it feels crunchy. To me, the best Pacific oysters taste like windswept ocean spray in the face – salty and irresistible.

We need salt. Every cell in our body contains salt and, besides, salt makes everything taste better. Try a simple experiment: fry two thin pieces of beef fillet, adding a little salt to one and not the other. Taste the unsalted one first. There's something not quite right, something missing. Now taste the other piece. That's much better. The flavour of the meat is rich and full. It just needed salt.

Salt goes with

Extra virgin olive oil as a dip for crudites such as carrot, cucumber, celery hearts and capsicum; buttered sourdough bread with thinly sliced radishes; a chicken (or duck), rubbed generously on its skin before roasting; wedges of ripe red tomatoes; cool cream of sorrel soup; a minute steak seared in just-smoking extra virgin olive oil for a few seconds a side.

Salt cod with green olives and capers

INGREDIENTS

750g piece of salt cod
extra virgin olive oil, for frying
1 onion, chopped
3 garlic cloves, peeled and sliced
180ml dry white wine
1 tbsp salted capers, rinsed well
1 cup green olives, pitted and chopped
salt and pepper

METHOD

- Soak piece of salt cod (also called baccala) in plenty of fresh water for 24 hours, changing the water every 8 hours or so. Drain well and pat dry. Cut into eight roughly even pieces.
- Heat a little extra virgin olive oil in a pan and lightly fry chopped onion and sliced garlic for 5 minutes. Add the salt cod pieces and fry for 3 minutes on each side. Pour in dry white wine, well-rinsed salted capers and pitted and chopped green olives. Simmer for 15-20 minutes until the cod is tender. Season with salt and pepper and serve.

Serves 4

Florentine-style salt cod

INGREDIENTS

800g salt cod, rehydrated and desalted, cut into bite-sized pieces
80g plain flour
10 tbsp extra virgin olive oil
4 medium-sized waxy potatoes, peeled and cut into 1cm-thick rounds
500g ripe tomatoes, chopped
2 garlic cloves, peeled and chopped
¼ cup chopped parsley, chopped fine
salt and pepper

METHOD

- Pat dry the pieces of salt cod and dust them with the flour. Heat half the olive oil in a pan and fry the salt cod on all sides till golden. Place on kitchen paper to drain. Fry the potato slices in the same oil until golden. Arrange the potatoes and salt cod pieces in a pan and scatter the garlic slices over. Add the chopped tomatoes, sprinkle with the remaining olive oil and season with pepper. Bring to a simmer and keep cooking for 15-20 minutes.
- Add the parsley and cook for a minute or two more. Check for salt and adjust if necessary. Serve hot.

Serves 4

Whole morwong baked in a salt crust

INGREDIENTS

650-800g whole white-
    fleshed flaky fish, gutted
    with scales left on
salt and pepper
300-400g coarse sea salt
extra virgin olive oil
lemon or lime juice

METHOD

- Any white-fleshed, flaky fish such as sea bream, snapper, pearl perch or sea perch will do. Leave it whole and have it gutted, but it's important to leave the scales on as they will protect the flesh from the salt. Season the cavity of the fish with salt and pepper.
- Preheat the oven to 190C. Place coarse sea salt in a baking dish and lay the fish on top. Completely cover the fish with more sea salt so there are no exposed areas. Drizzle some water gently on the salt and place in the oven for 30 minutes or more, depending on the size of the fish.
- Remove the dish from the oven and crack the salt crust at the table, pushing it aside to reveal the skin. The skin will peel off very easily to reveal the flesh.
- Drizzle with extra virgin olive oil and lemon or lime juice and serve.

Serves 2

CURRANT GRAPES

You may have seen those cute, tight little bunches of miniature grapes in the shops. They make an all-too-brief appearance as if to announce the start of the table grape season.

They're not the same fruit as the red, white and black fresh currants that bear only a bunching resemblance to grapes. Those tri-coloured fresh currants are a relative of the gooseberry rather than the grape.

Our interest is in the pea-sized grapes and, while much of the harvest is used for dried currants, more is sold each year as fresh fruit. The taste is intensely sweet with a lively acidity to balance, making them a natural accompaniment to a wide range of table cheeses.

Their ancient relatives are Greek. They are known as black corinthian or zante grapes. After sultanas, they are the second most important for drying but, as fresh fruit, currant grapes are versatile. The most obvious is as part of a dessert, as a topping for a custard tart or in a trifle.

Their keen acidity renders them suitable as a counterpoint to rich meats such as duck, pork, venison and quail. Sean's Panaroma restaurant at Bondi Beach in Sydney serves corn-fed duck salad with romano lettuce hearts, snake beans and currant grapes. In this dish, they provide visual appeal as well as a foil for the duck.

A very simple way to prepare them is to roast them in a hot oven, preferably wood-fired for better flavour. Lay the whole bunches on a roasting tray, drizzle with extra virgin olive oil and place in a preheated oven at 250C for 8-10 minutes until they are just about to burst. Serve as an accompaniment to roast meat.

Pickled currant grapes

INGREDIENTS

800g fresh currant grapes on stems
3 cups red wine vinegar
¼ cup sugar
2 whole cloves
1 allspice berry (or 4 whole black peppercorns)

METHOD

- This recipe is adapted from *Chez Panisse Fruit* by Alice Waters.
- Keep the currants on the stems, wash well and dry carefully, making sure they don't bruise. Bring vinegar, sugar, allspice and cloves to boil and turn down to simmer for 5 minutes. Let cool.
- Pack currant bunches carefully into preserving jars with self-sealing lids according to manufacturer's instructions. Pour cooled liquid over fruit and seal. Store in cool, dark place for six weeks before serving.
- Can be used as accompaniment to roast pork, game birds and meat.

Makes six 250ml jars

Currant grapes go with
Sugar, especially brown, rock and demerara; whipped cream; mascarpone and clotted cream; custard; puff pastry; sponge cake; aged balsamic vinegar; aniseed; cinnamon; star anise; clove; nutmeg; nuts, especially hazelnut, walnut and almond; game meats such as venison, quail, pigeon and guineafowl; rich meats such as oxtail, pork and terrines; most cheeses.

Pan-fried quails with spinach and currant grapes

Currant grapes in grape jelly

INGREDIENTS

2kg white grapes

white sugar (see method for exact quantities)

1 cup currant grapes, off the stem

METHOD

🍽 Juice the white grapes and strain the liquid through muslin. Measure the juice and put it into a saucepan. For every litre of juice add 300g of sugar. Bring to the boil and stir so the sugar dissolves. Skim off any muck that develops on the surface. Keep boiling until it has reduced by a third. Cool a little, then ladle into soup bowls or glass dessert goblets.

🍽 Place in the fridge for 15 minutes then add some of the currant grapes to each bowl.

Serves 8

INGREDIENTS

4 large quails

3 tbsp extra virgin olive oil

2 garlic cloves, minced

1 small onion, finely diced

100g spinach leaves, washed

salt and pepper

½ cup currant grapes, taken off stem

2 tsp good quality balsamic vinegar

METHOD

🍽 With a small, sharp knife, take legs off each quail at thigh joint and cut eight breasts off, leaving quail frame (can be used to make stock).

🍽 In a wide frypan, heat olive oil until very hot. Sprinkle quail legs and breasts with salt and fry until skin is crisp (about 2 minutes each side). Remove quails, add a little more olive oil to the pan if necessary and lightly fry garlic and onion for a minute. Add spinach leaves and fry lightly until just wilted. Season with salt and pepper, add currant grapes and balsamic vinegar.

🍽 Mix gently and serve spinach with quails on top.

Serves 4

WINTER

JERUSALEM ARTICHOKES

The Jerusalem artichoke is neither an artichoke nor is it from Jerusalem. It's really a tuber, like a potato or a yam. The name appears to have a convoluted origin and I'm yet to find a satisfactory explanation for the Jerusalem part of it. To my mind they taste nutty, like Brazil nuts, chestnuts or hazelnuts. Their flavour is more reminiscent of a cardoon – a close relative of the globe artichoke – than of artichoke itself.

Soup is one of the easiest ways to use it. Peel and slice the tubers, then lightly fry in butter or olive oil with a finely sliced onion. Add vegetable or chicken stock, your favourite herbs and simmer for about half an hour or until tender. Season, then puree and serve.

Jerusalem artichokes contain copious amounts of iron – five times that of potatoes and comparable to the iron content of red meat – so vegetarians please take note. Because of their iron content, they discolour quickly once peeled. Lemon juice helps maintain colour, but if it is added to the water at the start of cooking, the tubers have a tendency to stay a little firm. If you want them soft, add the lemon juice a couple of minutes before the end of the cooking time.

What to look for

With Jerusalem artichokes, the plumper they are the better – there will be fewer knobbly bits to discard. A good trick to determine flavour is to nibble on one. Avoid those that are soft or sprouting. Choose those of similar size as this will ensure they cook evenly. They're at their best from autumn through winter. Their quality declines as spring arrives.

Jerusalem artichokes go with

Butter; extra virgin olive oil; vinegar; mustard; onions; garlic; parsley; chives; coriander; thyme; spinach and silver beet; potatoes; celery; roast tomatoes; anchovies; scallops; prawns; meaty fish such as bar cod, blue eye and snapper; baccala (salt cod); veal; beef; chicken; kangaroo; venison; duck.

Jerusalem artichokes with cream of bagna cauda

INGREDIENTS

100g unsalted butter
100ml extra virgin olive oil
3 garlic cloves, minced
8 anchovy fillets, roughly chopped
50ml cream
salt
½ tsp potato flour
400g Jerusalem artichokes, peeled and thinly sliced
1 litre milk
juice of ½ lemon

METHOD

🍽 Place the butter, olive oil and garlic in a saucepan and heat on a low flame until the garlic cooks but does not colour – about 8 minutes. Turn off the heat and add the anchovy fillets. Mix with a wooden spoon until the anchovies have dissolved. Add the cream and salt to taste. Add the potato flour and whisk well with a fork or small whisk. Put the sliced Jerusalem artichokes and milk in a pot with the lemon juice and simmer for 6-7 minutes till the slices are tender.

🍽 Drain carefully and arrange the slices in layers in a baking dish. Pour the bagna cauda cream on top. Place in a preheated 200C oven for 6-8 minutes till golden.

Serves 4

Roasted Jerusalem artichokes

INGREDIENTS

750g Jerusalem artichokes
4-5 tbsp extra virgin olive oil
salt and pepper

METHOD

🍽 Wash Jerusalem artichokes. Preheat the oven to 350C. Place the artichokes in a baking pan with extra virgin olive oil and toss so they are coated. Season with salt and pepper. Roast for 10 minutes, then toss and return to the oven for 10 minutes. Check them with a sharp knife – they should pierce easily.

🍽 Serve hot as an accompaniment to roasts or grilled fish.

Serves 8

Grilled Jerusalem artichoke, red onion and olive salad

INGREDIENTS

8 plump Jerusalem artichokes

3 red onions

2 tbsp extra virgin olive oil

balsamic vinegar

salt and pepper

1 bunch watercress

1 cup small green or black olives

½ cup roughly chopped flat-leaf parsley

vinaigrette for dressing

METHOD

- Wash plump Jerusalem artichokes, leaving them unpeeled. Add them to cold, salted water in a pot and bring to the boil, simmering until they are al dente – tender but still a little firm. Cool and cut lengthways into 8mm-thick slices. Skin and quarter red onions, toss them in extra virgin olive oil and a good splash of balsamic vinegar. Season with salt and pepper and roast in a 220C oven until soft. Remove from the oven and cool.
- Grill the slices on a barbecue or griddle pan for a minute on each side. In a big bowl, mix the onions, watercress, small green or black olives and roughly chopped flat-leaf parsley.
- Add the hot, grilled artichokes and season, dress with vinaigrette.

Serves 4

PORK

Is the pork you're buying lacking flavour? Is it dry – even when you flash a thin slice of loin in a hot pan with some oil? Chances are the pork you've bought is lacking fat.

When it comes to pork, tenderness, juiciness and flavour can be elusive if the meat doesn't have enough fat. Without it, most meats – especially the primary cuts destined for the pan, grill or barbecue – turn out dry, tough and tasteless. Growth hormones, used legally by some pig farmers, turn fat into muscle, producing a leaner animal but effectively reducing flavour.

Pino Tomini Foresti knows pork. People travel from all over Sydney to Pino's in Kogarah to buy his pork. He uses Bangalow Sweet Pork exclusively because it is hormone- and antibiotic-free and has been allowed to develop the all-important fat around and within the muscles.

Tomini Foresti says: "I won't buy any pig that doesn't have at least 1½ to 2 fingers [16-20mm] of fat around the loin because it has no flavour."

Clayton Wright concurs. His father's shop, Terry Wright Butchery, has been a Randwick, Sydney, institution for half a century. Clayton sells the Berkshire Black pig under the brand Kurobuta Pork. He says: "The Kurobuta has a similar amount of fat around the loin, but also has marbling through the muscles, which gives it a sweet flavour."

Crumbed pork on a stick

INGREDIENTS

pork chops
plain flour
beaten egg
breadcrumbs
grated parmesan
handful of roughly chopped
    fresh sage
salt and pepper
1 tbsp butter
1 tbsp extra virgin olive oil

METHOD

🍴 Allow one pork chop per person. Beat the flesh as flat as possible using a meat hammer, taking care not to separate it from its rib. Dust each flat chop with flour, then dip in some beaten egg and finally crust it in a mixture of two-thirds breadcrumbs and a third grated parmesan, a good handful of roughly chopped fresh sage, salt and pepper to taste.

🍴 Heat a tablespoon each of butter and extra virgin olive oil in a large pan and lightly fry on both sides until golden.

🍴 Serve with a wedge of lemon.

Serves 1

What to look for
Meat that is guaranteed to be free of growth hormones and antibiotics. Always ask for meat from a sow (female) as boars (males) tend to have an unpleasant smell and can be tough. As well as the brands mentioned, Gungel Farm Pork is excellent. Buy chops with the fat still on. Don't overcook chops, loin or fillet because the meat will toughen.

Pork goes with
Extra virgin olive oil; vinegar; tomatoes; chillies; relish and chutney; star anise; garlic; onions; shallots; tomatoes; fennel; ginger; polenta; parsnips; mustard; soy sauce; potatoes; herbs such as sage, rosemary and parsley; apples; pears; prunes; lentils.

Pork knuckle with lentils

INGREDIENTS

pork knuckles

2 carrots, chopped

2 onions, chopped

parsley stalks

2 celery sticks

8-10 whole peppercorns

2 cups lentils

1.5 litres chicken or veal stock

1 celery heart, finely chopped

4 garlic cloves, minced

1 onion, finely diced

1 carrot, finely diced

½ cup chopped parsley

salt and pepper

METHOD

🍽 Allow one pork knuckle per person. Wash well and dry completely with kitchen paper. Place the knuckles in a large pot with a chopped carrot, an onion, a few parsley stalks, a couple of sticks of celery and 8-10 whole peppercorns. Simmer on a low heat, covered, for 2½ hours or until the knuckles are tender.

🍽 Meanwhile, wash lentils and place them in a pot with chicken or veal stock, a finely chopped celery heart, minced garlic cloves, a finely diced onion, a finely diced carrot and a good pinch of salt, and bring to a boil. Reduce the heat and simmer until just cooked – about 25 minutes.

🍽 When done, mix in parsley. Season with salt and pepper and serve with the pork knuckle.

Serves 8

Pork ragu for spaghetti

INGREDIENTS

6 tbsp extra virgin olive oil

100g pancetta, sliced and chopped fine

1 celery heart, finely chopped

1 carrot, finely chopped

1 onion, finely chopped

750g pork neck, minced

1.5kg ripe tomatoes, skinned and pureed

1 tbsp tomato paste

sprig rosemary, chopped

1 cup chopped parsley

salt and pepper

METHOD

🍽 Heat the olive oil in a saucepan and add the pancetta, carrot, onion, and celery. Stir on moderate heat for a minute or so. Add the minced pork neck. Stir until the meat has browned – about 5 minutes. Add the tomato paste and the rosemary and stir well.

🍽 Now add the tomatoes and keep simmering for 70 minutes or so till the sauce is thick. Add the parsley and season with salt and pepper.

Makes enough ragu for 8-10

TUNA

Fluctuations in the price of tuna can be hard to fathom. Yellowfin, for example, can rise from a low of about $20 a kilogram to well over $40.

Three variables determine the cost: availability, species and quality from fish to fish. Availability is linked to the moon's phases. Tuna swim close to the surface, where they feed on fish, krill and squid. The moon's light attracts tuna by illuminating their favourite food. If there is no moon, the tuna can't find their food thus most tuna boats don't fish between the new moon and the first quarter. At that time of the month, what is available is usually very expensive.

Yellowfin tuna is the species that tends to be available but we don't see the very best in our markets. These are reserved for export to Japan where they fetch astronomical prices. Southern bluefin and bigeye can sell for hundreds of dollars a kilogram in Japan for the sashimi market.

Still, tuna is so deliciously versatile that even the underrated albacore can be prepared so that it eats well above its class. I don't know why it's not more widely available. Try putting fresh albacore tuna in an oven dish and covering with a mixture of pureed tomatoes, fresh basil, chopped chilli, a couple of minced garlic cloves, extra virgin olive oil, salt and pepper. Cook in the oven on about 130C for about 45-50 minutes. When ready, cool and then pull the tuna apart with a fork and serve on grilled slices of bread.

Sweet and sour tuna

INGREDIENTS
1kg onions
4 tbsp extra virgin olive oil
1 cup water
4 tbsp sugar
pinch salt, plus extra for seasoning
250ml white wine vinegar
6 tuna steaks
plain flour, for dusting

METHOD
- Peel and finely slice onions and gently fry in extra virgin olive oil for 5 minutes, stirring continually. Add a cup of water, turn up the heat a little and simmer till all the liquid has evaporated. Dissolve sugar and salt in a bowl with white wine vinegar. Add to the onions, bring to the boil, and then take off the heat and season with salt only.
- Meanwhile, lightly flour six tuna steaks and pan-fry quickly so that they're still a little underdone in the middle. Place on serving plates and cover each steak with the hot sweet and sour onions.
- Let them cool before serving with chopped fresh mint.

Serves 6

What to look for
Yellowfin tuna selected from larger fish will be the most expensive. Select a fish of even colour and clear unblemished flesh. The most highly prized part of the tuna is the belly. It is the fattiest part of the fish and is best for eating raw or quick grilling.

Tuna goes with
Extra virgin olive oil; mayonnaise; eggs; soy sauce; wasabi; radish, especially daikon; onions; garlic; tomatoes; capers; herbs, especially basil, coriander, fennel, oregano and parsley; spices, especially cumin, pepper, paprika, cayenne and ginger; olives; rice; pasta; bread; pancetta; prosciutto; peas; beans; waxy potatoes; cabbage; radicchio, treviso.

Calabrian-style grilled tuna

Tuna tartare

INGREDIENTS

80g seedless raisins

800g tuna fillet, bloodline removed

10 anchovies, drained and finely chopped

80g pinenuts, toasted and roughly chopped

1 tbsp capers, well rinsed and chopped

6 tbsp extra virgin olive oil

salt and pepper

METHOD

🍽 This recipe has been adapted from a dish by a favourite osteria (traditional restaurant) in Milan – Osteria Grand Hôtel.

🍽 Place the raisins in a bowl and cover with tepid water for 30 minutes. Drain and pat them dry. Meanwhile, cut the tuna carefully in 5mm cubes and place in a bowl. Chop the raisins and add to the tuna along with the anchovies, pinenuts, capers and olive oil. Mix well and season to taste with salt and pepper.

🍽 Cover with cling film and refrigerate for an hour. Serve on individual plates on some finely sliced, peppery rocket leaves.

Serves 6

INGREDIENTS

6 tbsp extra virgin olive oil

1 onion, finely chopped

3 garlic cloves, minced

8 anchovies, chopped

150g button mushrooms, sliced

300g ripe tomatoes, chopped

2 sprigs fresh oregano, chopped

150g pitted black olives

250g drained tinned tuna

½ cup chopped flat-leaf parsley

salt and pepper

METHOD

🍽 In a pan, heat extra virgin olive oil and lightly fry finely chopped onion, minced garlic cloves, chopped anchovies and sliced button mushrooms for 4-5 minutes till soft. Add chopped, ripe tomatoes, chopped fresh oregano and pitted black olives, simmering for 5 minutes more. Add drained, tinned tuna and flat-leaf parsley, simmering for 15-20 minutes, stirring until the tuna has broken up.

🍽 Season with salt and pepper and serve with grilled fresh tuna steaks.

Makes enough sauce for 10 or more

BARLEY

To warm the cockles, I propose we use more barley during the cold winter months.

I won't bore you with the many proven benefits this grain has for our wellbeing because after you've eaten the quick and easily prepared lamb shank and barley stew, you, your friends and family will have ingested more goodies than any vitamin supplements could provide.

Barley is easy to use, readily available and a little goes a long way. Look for "pearl" or "pearled" barley. Before cooking, wash it well in cold water. There's no need to soak it overnight as it cooks relatively quickly. It can be prepared al dente by throwing a cupful into boiling salted water for 30-40 minutes. Drain and dress simply with a little butter or olive oil or any sauce you would normally use to accompany pasta or couscous.

Barley goes with

Butter; extra virgin olive oil; chicken, veal, lamb or vegetable stock; lamb or veal shanks; braised meats such as ossobuco, pork neck or shoulder and duck legs; onion; garlic; tomato; pumpkin; potato; carrot; celeriac; Jerusalem artichokes; spinach; parsley; sage; thyme; oregano.

Seafood and barley soup

INGREDIENTS

250g pearled barley
4 tbsp extra virgin olive oil
4 shallots, peeled and sliced thinly
3 garlic cloves, peeled and crushed
½ tsp smoked paprika
1 cup dry white wine
3 litres water
2 cups tomato passato (puree)
3 banana chillies, seeded and quartered lengthways
300g shelled peas
500g shelled medium king prawns, deveined
16 scallops
500g calamari, cut into 2cm tiles
500g clams, well washed
300g fish fillet, cut into 3cm pieces
1 cup chopped parsley
salt and pepper

METHOD

🍽 Place the barley in a sieve and wash quickly under running water to remove any dust or dirt. Heat the olive oil in a large pot and gently fry the shallots, garlic and paprika for a minute. Add the wine, turn up the heat and boil until there is almost no liquid left. Add the water and the passato, and the banana chillies. Bring to the boil and add the barley. Simmer for 15 minutes then add the peas. Simmer for 15 minutes more then add the seafood. Cook for 5 minutes then add the parsley.

🍽 Season with salt and pepper to taste and stir well. Serve hot

Serves 8

Note: Leftover stew can be excellent a day or two after being made though the barley will have absorbed all the liquid. Reheat by adding a cup of water and ¼ cup of tomato puree and gently bringing to the boil. More prawns or other seafood can be added to make a substantial "leftovers" meal.

Lamb shank and barley stew

INGREDIENTS

3-4 tbsp extra virgin olive oil

2 onions, chunkily chopped

8 garlic cloves, each cut into
    3-4 pieces

3 lamb shanks

4 carrots

300g pumpkin

300g celeriac (optional)

3 good pinches of salt

2 bay leaves

150g pearled barley

200g ripe tomatoes, chopped

salt and pepper

METHOD

🍴 This recipe makes enough for 4-6 people but it's a good idea to make double this amount as the stew is better the day after.

🍴 In a large soup pot, heat extra virgin olive oil and lightly fry chunkily chopped onions and garlic for a minute. Trim the fatty skin from lamb shanks and fry on moderate heat with the onions. Stir until the shanks have browned a little. Add, peeled and chopped in bite-sized chunks: carrots, pumpkin and celeriac (optional). Stir well for 30 seconds and cover with water. Add pinches of salt and bay leaves. Bring to boil, turn down to a simmer and cover for 40 minutes until shanks are tender.

🍴 Remove the shanks from the stew and add pearled barley and chopped, ripe tomatoes. Simmer for another 30-40 minutes. Strip the meat from the shanks and return to the soup.

🍴 Season with salt (if needed) and pepper and serve with plenty of grated parmesan.

Serves 4-6

Barley cooked like risotto

INGREDIENTS

150g pearled barley

1 carrot, peeled

½ celery heart

1 garlic clove

1 onion

3 tbsp extra virgin olive oil

3-4 ladles chicken or vegetable stock

handful chopped parsley

salt and pepper

METHOD

🍴 This is a perfect accompaniment to grilled or roasted meats, grilled veal or duck livers or hearty pork sausages. Soak 150g of pearled barley in cold water for 30 minutes.

🍴 In a food processor, or with a large knife, finely chop peeled carrot, celery heart, clove of garlic and onion. Fry lightly in extra virgin olive oil for 3-4 minutes until soft.

🍴 Add the (drained) barley and stir well through the vegetables. Add hot chicken or vegetable stock and simmer until the barley is tender. Add more stock if needed.

🍴 When cooked, add a handful of chopped parsley, season with salt and pepper and serve.

Serves 4

CARROTS

The carrot is part of the holy trinity of winter vegetables that includes onion and celery. These three form an indispensable cluster that gives slow cooking its foundation flavours.

In a stock, the carrot's flavour is extracted over many hours until finally, limp and spent, it is discarded. It fares better in soup – cooked until tender but still retaining some of its texture; nothing is wasted. But one of my favourite ways with carrots is with a slow-cooked, classic braising cut of meat, such as beef cheek or blade, in red wine. In this case, everything benefits from marinating overnight in a robust red wine: carrots (plenty of these, cut fairly large), celery, onion, garlic and trimmed beef cheeks.

The next day, drain the wine, brown the cheeks in a little oil, toss in the marinated vegetables and lightly fry. Add the wine so that the cheeks are almost covered and simmer for 90 minutes or more until the cheeks are tender.

Carrots go with
Butter; extra virgin olive oil; herbs such as parsley, rosemary, coriander, mint and thyme; cumin; pepper; turmeric; paprika; onions; garlic; celery; ginger; lemon; orange; fennel; radish; anchovies; walnuts; hazelnuts; pinenuts; almonds; raisins and currants.

Roast carrots with garlic and herbs

INGREDIENTS
¼ cup extra virgin olive oil
800g large carrots
15 large garlic cloves
salt
½ cup mixed fresh herbs (such as parsley, sage, thyme and coriander)
freshly ground pepper

METHOD
🍽 This is a perfect accompaniment to roast lamb or pork.

🍽 In a large roasting pan place extra virgin olive oil. Peel and cut large carrots into 4-5cm-long chunks and place in the pan. Add cloves of garlic, peeled but left whole. Salt the carrots and garlic well and toss in the olive oil so everything is coated.

🍽 Place in a preheated 220C oven for 20 minutes, remove from the oven and toss the carrots in their oil. Return to the oven and cook for another 10-15 minutes until they have charred a little.

🍽 Meanwhile, finely chop mixed fresh herbs. When the carrots are done, mix in the pan with the herbs, adding freshly ground pepper.

🍽 Serve hot in a bowl.

Serves 4-6

Braised carrots with cumin

Cream of carrots

INGREDIENTS

50g butter

600g carrots, peeled and thinly sliced into rounds

100g potatoes, peeled and thinly sliced

1 onion, peeled and thinly sliced

1 litre vegetable or chicken stock

100ml extra virgin olive oil

salt and pepper

METHOD

🍽 Heat the butter in a pot and fry the carrots, potatoes and onion for 3-4 minutes, continually stirring. Add the stock and simmer for 40 minutes till the vegetables are tender. Season with salt and pepper. Remove from the heat, add the olive oil and blitz to a puree or pass through a sieve.

🍽 Check for seasoning and serve as an accompaniment to grilled meats, fish or on toasted slices of crusty bread.

Serves 4

INGREDIENTS

700g carrots

salt

2 garlic cloves, minced

2 heaped tsp cumin seeds

extra virgin olive oil

½ cup water

1 short celery stalk

parsley stalks

coriander stalks

sprigs fresh thyme

juice of 2 oranges

METHOD

🍽 This dish is adapted from a recipe by Joel Robuchon.

🍽 Peel carrots and cut into 5mm-thick rounds. Place them in a large bowl, salt them well and add garlic cloves, cumin seeds and a couple of good splashes of extra virgin olive oil. Mix well.

🍽 Place everything into a braising pan and add water. Make a little bundle by tying a short length of celery, some parsley and coriander stalks and fresh thyme sprigs together. Mix this bundle into the carrots and cook on medium heat for 20 minutes, stirring occasionally. Add the orange juice and continue simmering for another 10 minutes until the carrots are tender.

🍽 Adjust the seasoning and serve with roast veal or chicken or as part of a banquet.

Serves 4

BROCCOLI

In 1992, United States president George Bush (senior) decreed broccoli would no longer be served to him at the White House.

He was asked about this at a state dinner for the Polish prime minister and replied, "Just as Poland had a rebellion against totalitarianism, I am rebelling against broccoli and I refuse to give ground. I do not like broccoli, and I haven't liked it since I was a little kid and my mother made me eat it. And I'm President of the United States and I'm not going to eat any more broccoli."

Some days later, California's broccoli growers sent the White House 10 tonnes of broccoli. The president was unmoved, saying, "Barbara loves broccoli. She's tried to make me eat it. She eats it all the time herself. So she can go out and meet the caravan."

A week later, Johns Hopkins University researcher Dr Paul Talalay published results showing broccoli contains a compound called sulforaphane, which helps to protect cells from damage and inhibits cancer. The research made headlines all over the world on the back of the president's petulant remarks and broccoli consumption rose dramatically.

Broccoli goes with
Butter; extra virgin olive oil; cream; eggs; cheeses, especially gruyere, cheddar, pecorino and parmesan; onions; chillies; garlic; ginger; capers; anchovies; pinenuts; almonds; soy sauce; fish sauce; tofu; rice; pasta; orange, lime and lemon juice; parsley; coriander; cumin; pastry and breadcrumbs.

Broccoli and ricotta sformato with taleggio sauce

INGREDIENTS

200g broccoli, trimmed of their woody bottoms
200g ricotta
1 egg
25g parmesan, finely grated
100g taleggio
salt and pepper

METHOD

🍽 Taleggio is a washed rind cheese from the Italian region of Lombardy. It is available at most good cheese shops.

🍽 Bring a pot of salted water to the boil and cook the broccoli till tender. Drain, take half the broccoli and chop it fine. Add the chopped broccoli to the ricotta, along with the egg, season with salt and pepper and mix well. Butter a mould and spoon in the mixture. Place in a preheated 160C oven for 20 minutes.

🍽 Meanwhile, pass the other half of the cooked broccoli through a sieve and put into a small pot. Chop the taleggio into small cubes and add to the sieved broccoli. Place the saucepan on a low heat and stir until the cheese has melted completely.

🍽 Remove the sformato from the oven and let it sit for 5 minutes before turning out and serving with the taleggio sauce.

Serves 4

Broccoli and gruyere tart

Long-cooked broccoli

INGREDIENTS

1kg broccoli

8 garlic cloves, peeled and thinly sliced

2 cups water

½ cup extra virgin olive oil

½ tsp dried chilli flakes

salt and pepper

3 anchovies, chopped

juice of 1 lemon

METHOD

🍽 This recipe is adapted from the book *Chez Panisse Vegetables* by Alice Waters.

🍽 Peel the tough outer skin from the stems of the broccoli. Slice the broccoli lengthways, about 5mm thick. Put the slices in a saucepan and add thinly sliced garlic, water, extra virgin olive oil and dried chilli flakes. Season with salt and pepper, bring to the boil and simmer for 50-60 minutes until the liquid is nearly evaporated.

🍽 Remove from the heat and add chopped anchovies and the juice of a lemon. Toss well. Serve hot on a platter with grated pecorino or parmesan.

Serves 6

INGREDIENTS

savoury shortcrust pastry

300g broccoli

250ml cream

2 eggs, well beaten

75g gruyere (or parmesan), grated

pinch salt

freshly ground pepper

METHOD

🍽 This delicious tart can be made in one 22cm-tart ring or several smaller ones. Line a tart ring with savoury shortcrust pastry and bake the shell until golden – this can be done the day before. Remove the florets from broccoli and pare back the tough outer skin from the stalks. Chop the stalks into thin rounds and blanch in salted boiling water, along with the florets, until tender. Drain well.

🍽 To make the filling, mix cream, well-beaten eggs, grated gruyere (or parmesan), pinch of salt and freshly ground pepper. Arrange the florets in the tart shell and scatter in the chopped stalks.

🍽 Pour in the cheese mixture and bake in a preheated 160C oven for 30 minutes, until it has just set. Cool a little before serving.

Serves 6

CELERIAC

If you're looking for cosmetic perfection celeriac may disappoint. It appears on fruiterers' shelves as a knobbly skinned ball with a twisted, beard-like tangle of roots at its base, often still clinging to bits of dry earth. But from winter to spring this Mediterranean vegetable will be pureed, roasted, braised, grilled, barbecued and eaten raw by a growing number of people who love its herbaceous, pungent flavour and versatility.

Perhaps its most famous use is in the French remoulade, a salad of raw strips of celeriac dressed with a rich mustard mayonnaise. Any assertive dressing will do as long as the celeriac is marinated in it for an hour or two to soften it and infuse the flavours.

Celeriac goes with
Mayonnaise; extra virgin olive oil; butter; cream and milk; parsley; fennel; chives; mustard; anchovies; olives; eggs; potatoes; lemon; chestnuts; most meats, especially chicken, rabbit, pork, beef and veal; white-fleshed fish, especially snapper, coral trout and dory; squid and cuttlefish.

Roast celeriac and gruyere tartlet

INGREDIENTS
savoury shortcrust pastry
1 medium-sized celeriac bulb
extra virgin oilve oil, for
    brushing
300ml milk
3 eggs, well beaten
handful chopped parsley
½ cup grated gruyere (or
    parmesan)
salt and pepper

METHOD
- Line one large (24cm) or eight small individual tart moulds with savoury shortcrust pastry. Pre-bake the shells. Peel the celeriac bulb and cut into discs about 1cm thick. Brush each disc with extra virgin olive oil, salt each side and bake in a preheated 190C oven for 25 minutes, turning once after 15 minutes so that both sides are golden. Cool a little after removing from the oven and cut each disc into 1cm cubes. Scatter the cubes evenly into the tart shells.
- Make the filling by combining milk with well-beaten eggs, chopped parsley, grated gruyere (or parmesan) cheese, salt and pepper. Mix well and pour into each tart shell to just below the edge. Bake in a preheated 180C oven until set, about 15-25 minutes depending on the size of the tart.
- Serve hot with a tossed salad.
Serves 8

Celeriac and chestnut soup

INGREDIENTS

800g trimmed celeriac bulbs

good pinch salt

20 chestnuts

150g butter

METHOD

🍽 Cut the trimmed celeriac into large, even chunks. Place in a pot big enough to hold the pieces. Cover with water and add salt. Place some silicone paper or a plate on top of the celeriac to keep the pieces submerged so they cook evenly. Bring to the boil then simmer until tender.

🍽 Meanwhile, preheat the oven to 200C. Score chestnuts by making a deep cross with a small, sharp knife on the flat side of each. Place on a baking tray and roast for 20-25 minutes. Remove from the oven and wrap in a clean tea towel for 5 minutes before peeling – this will help to loosen the fine inner skin. Once peeled, chop the chestnuts into rough pieces.

🍽 When the celeriac has cooked, remove from the water (don't throw the cooking water out) and place in a food processor. Add butter and puree the lot until smooth. If it is too thick, add some of the cooking water, season and the soup is ready.

🍽 To serve, ladle into individual bowls, adding pieces of chestnut, chopped fennel tips and finally a drizzle of olive oil.

Serves 6-8

Grilled scallops with celeriac remoulade

INGREDIENTS

200g celeriac, peeled and cut into matchstick-sized pieces

2-3 good pinches salt

100ml mayonnaise

1 tbsp seeded mustard

16 large scallops

2 tbsp extra virgin olive oil

4 tbsp parsley, finely chopped

salt and pepper

METHOD

🍽 Place the celeriac matchsticks in a bowl and toss with pinches of salt. Leave for 30 minutes, wash and pat dry.

🍽 Mix the celeriac sticks with the mayonnaise and mustard, seasoning with salt and pepper to taste. Leave for at least an hour.

🍽 Heat the olive oil in a pan. When it begins to smoke, add the scallops, one at a time, and cook on each side for 30-45 seconds to attain good colour. Add the chopped parsley to the celeriac and mix well.

🍽 Lay the remoulade on plates and serve the scallops on top.

Serves 4

CLEMENTINES

Clementines are a relatively new citrus fruit in Australia. Many fruiterers aren't aware they exist, but from Spain, Corsica and Italy to Morocco, Egypt and Algeria, across India, down the Malay Archipelago and up to China and Japan, the clementine is revered for its juicy, richly flavoured flesh and fragrant, deeply perfumed peel.

Clementines are a cross between the mandarin and the Seville orange. Mostly seedless and with bright red-orange skin, clementines are one of the smallest and sweetest fruits of the mandarin family. You'll find them available all winter through to early spring.

Clementines seem made for cold-weather snacking; they peel easily and have very little of the bitter "netting" attached to the segments. But they can be used in many ways. A combination of the tasty skin, cut into strips, and the juice makes a wonderful marmalade that is a perfect accompaniment for rich pork or duck dishes. Try tossing some clementine segments with thinly sliced fennel and then dressing with good olive oil, salt and pepper for an unusual winter salad.

Clementines go with
Cream and clotted cream; mascarpone; strawberries; mint; pineapple; passionfruit; chocolate; caramel; sugar; honey; sponge cake; puff pastry and sweet shortcrust pastry; almonds; hazelnuts; pistachios; pecans; kirsch; rum; Cointreau; grand marnier; grappa; duck; goose; lamb; pork.

Candied clementine peel

INGREDIENTS
6 clementines
sugar
water

METHOD
- Using a vegetable peeler or a sharp paring knife, peel strips of skin from clementines, taking care to remove as little as possible of the white pith immediately beneath the skin. Slice the strips thinly, add them to a pan of cold water and bring to the boil. Remove the peel from the heat, strain and run under cold water to refresh.
- Add the peel to a second pan of cold water and repeat the process.
- The third time, add half sugar, half water to just cover the peel and bring to a simmer. Keep simmering until the water reduces to a syrup.
- Store the candied peel in the syrup in a jar and place in the refrigerator.

Makes 250ml of peel

Clementine and hazelnut torta

INGREDIENTS

4 clementines

6 eggs

180g caster sugar

200g hazelnut meal

1 heaped tsp baking powder

METHOD

🍽 Put whole, unpeeled clementines in a pot of water and bring to the boil. Turn down the heat to a low simmer, cover and poach the clementines for 90 minutes. Remove them from the water and set them aside to cool. Trim off any woody end bits, cut each in half and remove any seeds.

🍽 Place the clementines in a food processor, skin and all, and pulse until pureed. Preheat the oven to 185C. Butter and lightly flour a 20cm-diameter cake tin. Whisk eggs in a bowl for 1 minute. Add caster sugar and whisk for 2-3 minutes until the sugar has lost its granular texture.

🍽 In a separate bowl, mix together hazelnut meal (not roasted) with baking powder. Add this to the wet mixture and whisk until well incorporated. Spoon the mixture into the cake tin and bake for 70 minutes.

🍽 Allow the cake to cool in the tin. To remove, run a knife around the edge. Serve with a dusting of icing sugar and some candied clementine peel.

Serves 10

Clementine curd

INGREDIENTS

6 clementines

3 tbsp water

100g sugar

115g unsalted butter, cut into small cubes

pinch salt

3 whole eggs

3 egg yolks

METHOD

🍽 Grate the zest from the clementines and keep for later. Squeeze enough juice from the clementines to give, when strained, 125ml. Put the juice in a stainless saucepan with the water, sugar, butter and salt. Turn the heat to low and stir until the sugar has dissolved and the butter melts.

🍽 Whisk the eggs and egg yolks together in a bowl for a minute then slowly add the butter and sugar mixture whisking vigorously until well incorporated. Scrape the mixture back into the stainless saucepan and, on a low heat, cook and stir slowly until it thickens and coats the back of a spoon. Stir in the zest and pour into a container.

🍽 Place some cling film on the curd's surface to prevent skin forming and refrigerate overnight to set.

🍽 Good with scones, fruit toast, pastries and plain tea cakes.

Makes about 750ml of curd

KIDNEYS

Among my friends and acquaintances, I can count on one hand the people who like kidneys or, for that matter, offal in general. Countless food magazines, cooking shows and celebrity chefs seem to have a collective phobia when it comes to offal. They aren't very helpful to those of us who find such cuts sublime.

A generation ago, a contemporary restaurant menu was guaranteed to contain at least one dish featuring kidneys, tripe, sweetbreads or liver. Granted, these dishes were never among the big sellers on the menu, but they catered to a passionate and usually more appreciative diner. With the disappearance of these dishes from the restaurant repertoire goes the skill and ability to prepare them. It's no wonder a group of dedicated diners formed the Tripe Club of New South Wales.

Veal or calf's kidneys are among my favourite things to eat. A good butcher should have no trouble getting them for you. They are the size of a small clenched fist. Double this size and chances are the kidneys come from mature beef cattle and will tend toward toughness. They are better kept for braising in a steak and kidney pie.

Kidneys go with

Extra virgin olive oil; sesame oil; butter; cream; soy sauce; garlic; ginger; pepper; herbs such as parsley, rosemary, thyme and sage; red wine; sherry; marsala; Worcestershire sauce; mustard; chilli; cayenne pepper; vinegar, especially balsamic, cider and wine; spinach; mushrooms.

Barbecued kidneys with fresh herbs and balsamic vinegar

INGREDIENTS

8 veal kidneys (two per person)
1 cup chopped flat-leaf parsley
1 cup chopped rosemary
1 cup chopped sage
salt and pepper
extra virgin olive oil
balsamic vinegar

METHOD

🍽 Clean and trim the kidneys. Roughly chop together a cup each of flat-leaf parsley, rosemary and sage. Sprinkle salt and pepper on each kidney, as well as a little extra virgin olive oil. Press the chopped herbs on each side of each kidney. Prepare the flat grill of the barbecue by cleaning it well and heating some extra virgin olive oil. When hot, barbecue the kidneys once only on each side. Small ones should take 3-4 minutes and larger ones a little longer. When nearly done, splash each kidney with good balsamic vinegar.

🍽 Remove from the grill and slice each into five or six pieces. They should still be a little pink inside. Serve immediately with a finely sliced fennel salad or a celeriac remoulade.

Serves 4

Veal kidneys in red wine, parsley and garlic

Roast kidneys apicius-style

INGREDIENTS

4 lamb kidneys

½ tsp ground pepper

½ cup roasted almonds, finely chopped

1 tsp ground coriander

pinch ground fennel seed

2 tbsp extra virgin olive oil

salt

4 rashers of prosciutto, thinly sliced

METHOD

🍽 Trim the fat from the kidneys and cut lengthways without separating them. Spread them out on a board and fill them with the pepper, almonds, coriander, fennel seed and olive oil. Season lightly with salt and close the kidney halves together.

🍽 Wrap each kidney with the prosciutto and secure with toothpicks. Place in a baking tray and roast in a preheated 180C oven for 30 minutes.

🍽 Serve with polenta or couscous.

Serves 2

INGREDIENTS

8 small veal kidneys (two per person)

plain flour, for dusting

6 tbsp extra virgin olive oil

1 large or 2 small onions, chopped

4 garlic cloves, minced

1 cup dry red wine

½ cup chopped flat-leaf parsley

salt and pepper

METHOD

🍽 Trim small veal kidneys and cut into bite-sized pieces. Lightly dust them with plain flour. Heat extra virgin olive oil in a sauté pan. On moderate heat, fry chopped onions, minced garlic and the kidneys for 5 minutes. Stir constantly. Add dry red wine and cook until the liquid thickens and reduces to a sauce. It should take 4-5 minutes.

🍽 Turn off the heat, add chopped flat-leaf parsley, season with salt and pepper and serve the kidneys on toasted bread.

Serves 4

PEPPER

Go to any good Thai produce shop and you're likely to find fresh pepper. The densely packed berries are clustered around a central stem and look a little like peas, only a third the size.

Pick one, bite it and you'll get an instant burst of juice, laden with fruity, moderate heat. If allowed to dry, these berries darken and what's left is common black pepper.

Black pepper has a more intense "pepperiness" than green pepper due to a volatile oil called piperine, which forms in the outer husk as it dries.

I like to use fresh green peppercorns as much as possible while they're in season to liven up just about any sauce or dressing. Add them as whole berries to a pasta sauce. Grind them into a paste in a mortar with herbs such as parsley or coriander and some garlic. Dilute the paste with a little extra virgin olive oil, season with salt and you've got an all-purpose salsa for roast meat or grilled seafood.

A word of caution: the green peppercorns oxidise quickly once they're crushed, so it's a good idea to make the salsa and use it within the hour. If you can't find fresh pepper locally, it's worth a trip to Chinatown. Better still, ask your fruiterer to get some for you.

Peppered turnips baked with cheese

INGREDIENTS

500g turnips

mozzarella slices

salt and freshly cracked pepper

butter

freshly grated parmesan

METHOD

- This recipe is adapted from *The Original Mediterranean Cuisine* by Barbara Santich.
- Peel turnips and poach them whole in salted boiling water until just tender, then slice thinly (to about 3mm thickness).
- Butter an ovenproof dish and arrange the turnip slices in overlapping rows in one layer. Cut thin slices of mozzarella and tuck under every second row of turnips. Season well with lots of freshly cracked pepper and salt. Dot with butter and sprinkle with freshly grated parmesan. Cook under a grill or in an oven until brown.

Serves 6

Pepper goes with

All meats; fish and shellfish; onions; garlic; balsamic vinegar; soy sauce; red wine; port; poaching liquid for pears, apples, quinces and all stone fruit; strawberries; braised or fried mushrooms; stuffing for poultry; crusting for roasts; soups; salads; most cheeses, especially aged pecorino.

Pan-fried fresh peppercorn and garlic beef

Leek and peppercorn sauce

INGREDIENTS

2 eggs, hard boiled and chopped

1 tsp ground cumin

¼ tsp ground pepper

1 tbsp parsley, finely chopped

¼ cup leeks, tender white part finely sliced

6 peppercorns, coarsely ground

1 tbsp honey

1 tsp white wine vinegar

2 tbsp extra virgin olive oil

salt

METHOD

🍽 Mix the chopped, hard-boiled eggs with the pepper and cumin. Add the rest of the ingredients and mix well. Cover and set in the refrigerator.

🍽 Use as an accompaniment to braised meats such as lamb or beef casserole, ossobuco, braised lamb or veal shanks or as an addition to hearty soups such as lentils or oxtail.

Serves 6

INGREDIENTS

2 good pinches salt

¼ cup fresh peppercorns or 2 tsp dried peppercorns

4 garlic cloves, peeled

3 shallots, peeled and sliced

5 tbsp extra virgin olive oil

beef pieces, 1cm thick

2 tbsp olive oil

METHOD

🍽 In a mortar place salt, fresh peppercorns (or dried), peeled cloves of garlic and peeled and sliced shallots. Pound to a rough paste then add extra virgin olive oil and mix well.

🍽 Cut 1cm-thick pieces of beef – sirloin, fillet or rump. Heat olive oil in a pan and fry the beef slices on both sides. Place them on a warm serving plate and return the frypan to the heat, adding the peppercorn paste.

🍽 Gently fry the paste for 4-5 minutes, turn off the heat then return the beef slices to the pan and coat them with the paste. Serve immediately.

Serves 4

DESSERTS

For some, dessert is the business end of the meal. They'll tolerate – but only just – having to eat their greens so they can have the pudding. Winter is their time, when desserts get creamier, thicker and richer.

When we think of a rich dessert, many of us think of chocolate and a hot chocolate pudding, brought steaming from the oven. To get the most intense flavour, it's essential to use the best chocolate available. Compound chocolate won't do; it results in a papery, flat flavour. Use good couveture chocolate and your pudding and sauce will taste great.

Not quite as rich but just as satisfying is the monte bianco. Named after the mountain between France and Italy and shaped to resemble the famous peak, it is a classic dessert but not often seen on menus in Australia. It's easier to use frozen, peeled chestnuts but fresh chestnuts will do.

Along with chestnuts and quinces, pears make up my triumvirate of favourite winter fruits. These beurre bosc pears look stunning, especially when they're sliced. The ruby port gives them a wonderful colour and, steeped with spices, produces a fragrant sauce that is perfect accompanied simply with cream or icecream. Be sure to choose pears that are still a little firm so they keep their texture once poached.

To finish the quartet, the caramel kisses can be eaten at any time of day. For morning coffee or afternoon tea, they can take the place of biscuits or cake and will even stand in for petit fours after dinner.

Chocolate puddings with chocolate sauce

INGREDIENTS

250g butter
1½ cups caster sugar
1 tsp vanilla essence
zest of 2 lemons, grated
4 eggs
2 cups plain flour
50g Dutch cocoa
2½ tsp baking powder
pinch salt
250g dark couverture chocolate
¾ cup milk
250ml single cream
1 tbsp butter

METHOD

🍽 Cream butter and caster sugar. Add vanilla essence, the grated lemon zest, two whole eggs and two yolks (reserving the two whites). Sift plain flour, Dutch cocoa, baking powder and a pinch of salt and add to the mixture. Melt 50g of the dark couverture chocolate and mix in with the milk. Whisk the remaining two egg whites to soft peaks and fold into the mixture. Butter and sugar individual pudding (dariole) moulds. Fill with the mixture.

🍽 Place the puddings in a baking dish and pour boiling water into the dish so it comes two-thirds up the sides of the moulds. Bake at 180C for 30-35 minutes or until they feel firm to the touch.

🍽 To make the sauce, bring a half-filled pot of water to the boil, place a neatly fitting stainless-steel bowl on top containing remaining 200g of dark couverture chocolate, single cream and the tablespoon of butter. Turn the heat off immediately and, once everything melts, mix it well together so it becomes a glossy sauce.

🍽 Serve with the warm puddings.
Makes 12 puddings

Desserts go with
Dessert wines; fruit-based desserts call for lighter style dessert wines such as Moscato d'Asti or a late-picked riesling or semillon; cream- and custard-enriched cakes and pastries are good with auslese rieslings and not overly rich, partially botrytised semillon; rich desserts such as puddings with caramel, pralines and toffee call for richer wines like full-bodied botrytis semillon, riesling and sauternes; chocolate desserts are best with liqueur muscat or tokay, port or PX sherry.

Pears poached in ruby port

Monte bianco

INGREDIENTS
400g peeled chestnuts

500ml milk

200g sugar

2 split vanilla beans (or 1 tsp pure vanilla essence)

METHOD
🍽 Place peeled chestnuts in a saucepan, add milk, sugar and split vanilla beans (or pure vanilla essence). Simmer gently until the chestnuts are tender (this should take 1-1½ hours).

🍽 Allow the mix to cool. Remove the vanilla beans. Mash the chestnuts roughly with a fork. Pass the mix through a potato ricer to form long, spaghetti-like strands that pile over each other to form a mountain.

🍽 Serve in a pool of runny custard with a dollop of whipped cream on top and, finally, some grated dark chocolate.

Serves 4

INGREDIENTS
8 beurre bosc pears

750ml ruby port

2 cups verjuice

2 cups sugar

8 cardamom pods

1 cinnamon stick

3 whole cloves

6 whole peppercorns

3cm peeled fresh ginger, thinly sliced

METHOD
🍽 Peel the beurre bosc pears (the ones with a rusty-coloured skin) and arrange them in a pot so they fit snugly. Add ruby port, verjuice, sugar, cardamom pods, cinnamon stick, whole cloves, whole peppercorns and thinly sliced fresh ginger. Cut some silicone paper or "go-between" (similar to cellophane wrap) to fit over the pears, keeping them submerged; a plate can do the same job. Bring to boil and simmer gently till they're just cooked. Let the pears cool in the liquid.

🍽 Refrigerate overnight, keeping the paper on top (that will give them their unique colour).

🍽 Serve with vanilla gelato or freshly whipped cream.

Serves 8

BRAISING

Braising is a simple two-step process, first browning the food well in a pan and then adding liquid and gently simmering – never boiling – until done. The first results in desirable, dark caramel-like colours or crispness if skin is involved and the second draws out lip-smacking flavour by breaking down collagen and slowly melting sinew till tender. Beef cheeks are a classic example of this – a dish that makes your lips stick.

Because all that slow cooking tends to draw the sweeter flavours of the spectrum from meats and vegetables, we tend to use wine, vinegar or even verjuice for balance. Especially when braising vegetables such as fennel, a little vinegar adds a pleasant tang, complementing its sweet anise flavours.

Large octopus benefits greatly from slow braising and, even though it seems like very little liquid is added, its usually tough tentacles yield enough moisture to make a deliciously rich sauce.

Finally, the duck-leg dish highlights another braising tip – if you want the skin to stay relatively crisp, don't cover it with liquid. The resulting sauce should be flavoursome, but for more intensity, strain it, put it in a saucepan and turn up the heat until it reduces sufficiently.

Once you've gained confidence with the technique, braising is guaranteed to widen your cooking repertoire enormously.

Braising is good for
Secondary cuts of meat with a good amount of connective tissue; red and white wines; root vegetables such as carrots, shallots, onions, garlic, potatoes, turnips and leeks; celery; tomato puree; extra virgin olive oil; herbs such as parsley, sage, rosemary, thyme, coriander and basil.

Octopus braised in own juices

INGREDIENTS
- 2 large octopuses, about 500g each
- ¼ cup extra virgin olive oil
- 4 garlic cloves, peeled and sliced
- 1 tsp salted capers, well washed
- 10 olives, roughly chopped
- 4 anchovy fillets
- pinch salt
- 3 ripe tomatoes, roughly chopped
- 1 cup chopped parsley

METHOD
- Have your fishmonger clean the innards from the head of the octopus.
- Heat extra virgin olive oil in a big pan and add sliced garlic cloves, capers, roughly chopped olives and anchovy fillets. Stir for a minute. Add the octopus and a pinch of salt. Mix well, lower the heat, add ripe, roughly chopped tomatoes and chopped parsley.
- Cover tightly and cook very slowly for an hour till the octopus is tender.
- Serve with boiled potatoes.

Serves 5-6

Braised duck legs in red wine

INGREDIENTS
- 8 duck legs
- 4 tbsp olive oil
- 1 medium-sized onion, chopped
- few sprigs fresh rosemary
- 2 cups red wine
- 2 cups chicken stock
- salt

METHOD
- Salt the skin side of duck legs. Put them in a heavy skillet, skin side down, over moderate heat. As the skin browns, the fat will be rendered over 10-15 minutes. Make sure it doesn't burn.
- Remove the legs to a tray and discard fat. Heat olive oil in the same skillet and add chopped, medium-sized onion and a few sprigs of fresh rosemary. Lightly fry for 2-3 minutes then add red wine and chicken stock and bring to the boil.
- Arrange the legs, skin side up, in a braising pan and add enough of the boiling liquid so it leaves the skins exposed. Braise the legs in a 180C oven for about 75 minutes.

Serves 8

Braised beef cheeks with cannellini beans

INGREDIENTS

6 beef cheeks

plain flour, for dusting

olive oil

4 onions, diced

salt and pepper

3 carrots, peeled

10 garlic cloves, peeled

4 ripe tomatoes, peeled and
    pureed

dry white wine

1 tbsp plain flour

1 cup dried cannellini beans,
    soaked overnight

1 cup chopped parsley

METHOD

🍴 Allow a beef cheek per person, trimming each one of all
membranes. Dust them lightly with the plain flour. Heat some
olive oil in a skillet and brown the meat lightly. In a pot sauté
diced onions in a little olive oil making sure they become
transparent but don't colour. Arrange the cheeks on top of the
onions, season a little with salt and pepper, add carrots cut into
3cm lengths, whole peeled garlic cloves, peeled and pureed ripe
tomatoes and enough dry white wine so that the meat is almost
covered. Bring this to the boil, lower the heat and simmer,
covered, for 45 minutes.

🍴 Take half a cup of the liquid and mix with a tablespoon of plain
flour. Return this mixture to the pot, add cannellini beans, which
have been soaked overnight, and chopped parsley. Simmer for
another 45-60 minutes until the cheeks are tender.

🍴 Season and serve with freshly made polenta.

Serves 6

Braised fennel

INGREDIENTS

4 tbsp extra virgin olive oil

5 shallots, finely sliced

1 carrot, peeled and sliced

4 garlic cloves, chopped

2 good pinches salt

freshly ground pepper

2-3 bay leaves

3-4 sprigs fresh thyme

4 bulbs fennel

1 cup dry white wine

6 tbsp white wine vinegar

METHOD

🍴 Heat extra virgin olive oil in a high-sided
pan. Lightly fry finely sliced shallots,
peeled and sliced carrot and chopped
garlic cloves for 5 minutes till they
soften. Add a couple of good pinches
of salt, a few turns of fresh ground
pepper, bay leaves, sprigs of fresh thyme
and bulbs of fennel (with outer leaves
removed and sliced in half). Fry for 2
minutes more, stirring so the fennel is
well coated with the vegetables. Add dry
white wine and white wine vinegar and
season a little more. Bring to the boil
then place in a preheated 190C oven for
20-30 minutes till the fennel is tender
and can be pierced easily with a sharp
knife.

Serves 6

SOUPS

What better way to begin a winter feast than with a hearty soup? The basis of many winter soups is good stock. As our chicken and farro soup calls for pieces of diced chicken and chicken stock, it's a good idea to buy a whole chicken, trim the meat off and pop the carcass into a large pot. Add to this a chopped carrot, a chopped onion, a celery stalk and two cloves of garlic. Bring it to the boil, then turn it down to a simmer. Keep skimming the surface for any scum that develops and in two hours you have perfect, clear chicken stock. Use straight away or freeze for later.

This soup calls for farro (also called emmer), one of the ancient grains still grown in certain parts of the world. In Australia, it is grown in north-western NSW and can often be found in health or specialty stores. Farro adds great texture and heartiness as well as wonderful flavour.

Another unusual but increasingly sought-after ingredient, Tuscan kale – or cavolo nero, as it's known in Italy – combines with potato to produce a wonderfully thick soup. Unlike many greens, cavolo nero maintains its texture and increases its flavour as it cooks, resulting in a dense, meaty flavour.

For something different, the passato provides a change in texture. It's a smooth, velvety soup and can be made with almost any vegetable in season.

Finally, the fish stew uses an often-discarded part of large, white-fleshed fish – the cheek meat found in the head. This soup contains so much jelly that it usually sets when refrigerated overnight. This richness is what makes it so good.

Winter vegetable passato

INGREDIENTS

1 carrot
1 onion
1 celery heart
½ small butternut pumpkin
1 leek
2 potatoes
6 garlic cloves
250g savoy cabbage
1 cup shelled peas
150g broccoli
1 cup pure cream
salt and fine white pepper

METHOD

🍽 Peel (where necessary) and cut into chunks carrot, onion, celery heart, pumpkin, leek, potatoes, cloves of garlic, savoy cabbage, shelled peas and broccoli.

🍽 Place all the vegetables except the peas and broccoli in a large pot and just cover with cold water. Bring to the boil and simmer for 25 minutes. Add the remaining vegetables and simmer for a further 10 minutes.

🍽 Drain the cooked vegetables, setting the water aside, and pulse in a food processor until they are well blended. Add enough of the cooking water to give a rich, thick but runny consistency. Add pure cream, season with salt and fine white pepper and stir until uniform.

🍽 Reheat if necessary and serve in bowls with a drizzle of good extra virgin olive oil and fresh crusty bread or toasted bread with gruyere or cheddar melted on top.

Serves 6

Soups go with
Bread; croutons; crostini; toast; breadcrumbs; extra virgin olive oil; butter; cream; pesto; rouille; tarragon salsa; lemon; sherry; flaky salt; freshly cracked pepper; grated and shaved parmesan, gruyere and pecorino.

Chicken and farro soup

INGREDIENTS

¼ cup extra virgin olive oil

2 onions, diced

8 garlic cloves, sliced thickly

1 celery heart, sliced

3 fresh bay leaves

350g waxy potatoes, peeled and diced

250g ripe tomatoes, finely chopped

250g pearled farro (or barley)

chicken stock

2 good pinches salt

500g diced chicken thigh fillet

salt and pepper

METHOD

🍴 Heat extra virgin olive oil in a heavy-bottomed soup pot. Add diced onions, cloves of garlic sliced fairly thick, sliced celery heart (including the tender light-green leaves) and fresh bay leaves. Lightly fry the vegetables for 2-3 minutes, making sure they don't colour. Add peeled and diced waxy potatoes, finely chopped ripe tomatoes and stir.

🍴 Wash pearled farro (or barley), drain well and stir into the pot. Add enough chicken stock to cover everything by 3-4cm. Raise the temperature and bring to the boil. As soon as it boils, turn down to a simmer and add a couple of good pinches of salt. Keep simmering for 20-25 minutes until the farro softens. Add diced chicken thigh fillet and keep simmering until it is cooked.

🍴 Season with salt and pepper and serve.

Serves 8-10

Fish stew

INGREDIENTS

3kg fresh fish heads (bar cod, snapper, red emperor)

1 onion

1 carrot

1 celery heart

4 garlic cloves, minced

6 tbsp extra virgin olive oil

2 cups pureed tomatoes

½ cup roughly chopped parsley

salt and pepper

METHOD

🍴 You will need whole fresh fish heads – bar cod, snapper, red emperor or similar (not oily fish such as salmon or tuna) – scales off, gills out. Wash the fish heads well, place in a pot and just cover with cold water. Bring to the boil and turn down to a simmer for 30-40 minutes till cooked – skim off any scum floating on top. Let the heads cool in the water.

🍴 Drain (keep the stock), then remove the meat from the heads and reserve. Peel and chop onion, carrot, celery heart and garlic cloves and mince finely in a food processor. Heat extra virgin olive oil in a large pot and lightly fry the vegetables for 6-8 minutes. Add pureed tomatoes and roughly chopped parsley, then simmer for 25 minutes till all the flavours have mingled.

🍴 Add the broth and the fish head meat, bring back to a simmer, season with salt and pepper and serve.

Serves 6-8

ROASTS

The roast is one of the great showpieces of communal dining. Glistening with caramelised flesh, carved and served with classic accompaniments, the roast brings unity and focus to the winter meal.

Slow roasting results in a satisfying patina on flesh and is best with fattier, secondary cuts such as shoulders and necks. As these cook slowly over some hours, the fat melts, basting the meat, keeping it moist and tender. You'll find the pork neck deliciously tender and easily carved into neat rounds.

The veal nut is the opposite in almost every way to the pork neck. It comes from the leg, is lean, delicate in flavour and will dry out quickly if overcooked. It's best roasted at a high temperature for a relatively short time and allowed to "rest" once it comes out of the oven. For leaner cuts of meat especially, this resting time is important because it relaxes the muscle and allows the juices contained inside to "set" so that once it is sliced, those flavourful juices don't run everywhere. For a delicious variation, mash roast garlic into the pan juices to make a thick puree that will accompany the roast root vegetables.

Roasts go with

Potatoes; celeriac; parsnips; carrots; rosemary; sage; bay leaves; thyme; mushrooms; spinach; garlic; onions; red wine; braised lentils; steamed green beans with garlic and parsley; peas; crusty bread.

Roast veal nut with whole garlic cloves

INGREDIENTS

0.75-1.2kg veal nut
30 garlic cloves, peeled
extra virgin olive oil
salt and pepper
fresh rosemary

METHOD

- Have your butcher prepare a veal nut weighing between 0.75kg and 1.2kg. Peel garlic cloves, leaving them whole. Preheat the oven to 220C. Rub the veal nut well with extra virgin olive oil and season with salt and pepper. Sprinkle with fresh rosemary leaves – they should stick to the flesh. Lay in a roasting tray and place in the oven. After 10 minutes, add the garlic cloves around the roast and mix with a spoon so the garlic is well coated with the juices. Roast for another 15-20 minutes.
- Remove from the oven and rest for 10 minutes before slicing and serving.

Serves 3-4

Chinese roasted lamb racks

INGREDIENTS

½ cup honey
⅓ cup Chinese light soy
¾ cup minced fresh ginger
30 garlic cloves, finely diced
⅔ cup white sugar
⅔ cup black vinegar
3 cups shao hsing wine (Chinese cooking wine)
3 cups Chinese barbecue sauce
3 cups Chinese char siu sauce
3 tsp sesame oil
1 tbsp Chinese five-spice powder
6 lamb racks (each with 6 cutlets)

METHOD

- Kylie Kwong presented this dish at an Australia Day lunch in New York in 2002.
- Make a marinade with honey, Chinese light soy, ginger, garlic cloves, white sugar, black vinegar, Chinese cooking wine, Chinese barbecue sauce, char siu sauce, sesame oil and five-spice powder.
- Combine lamb racks with marinade in a bowl, cover and marinate in refrigerator overnight. Preheat oven to 240C, roast lamb cutlets for 5 minutes. Baste with generous amounts of the marinade, bake a further 8-10 minutes, or until medium-rare. Remove lamb from oven tray and rest for 10 minutes in a warm place. Glaze racks with a half-half mixture of honey and soy and serve.

Serves 6

Slow-roasted pork neck with sage

INGREDIENTS

1 pork neck side

salt and freshly cracked pepper

3 tbsp extra virgin olive oil

fresh sage, stalks left on

METHOD

🍽 Have your butcher prepare a pork neck side so that it includes four of the shoulder end ribs. Ask for these to be trimmed, the chine bone removed and the roast trimmed of excess knobs of fat. The remaining piece should weigh about 3kg and the ribs should be still attached but easily sliced off once roasted.

🍽 Sprinkle the roast with salt and freshly cracked pepper. Heat 3 tablespoons of extra virgin olive oil in a pan and brown the meat. In a roasting pan, lay a generous amount of fresh sage (leave stalk on) and the roast on top. Place in a 250C oven for 20 minutes then lower the temperature to 140C for 3 hours. Keep basting every 20 minutes or so.

Serves 6-8

Roast root vegetables

INGREDIENTS

3 carrots

3 parsnips

1 medium-sized celeriac root

12 plump Jerusalem artichokes

6 elephant garlic cloves

12 golf ball-sized beetroots

extra virgin olive oil

salt and pepper

fresh sprigs rosemary and sage

METHOD

🍽 Choose your favourite root vegetables – in this case, carrots, parsnips, celeriac root, Jerusalem artichokes, garlic cloves and beetroot. Peel all except the beetroot and cut into 2cm cubes, except the garlic, which is left whole.

🍽 Wash and scrub the beetroot well, trim the top, and place it, along with all the other vegetables, in a roasting pan. Toss with extra virgin olive oil, salt and pepper, fresh sprigs of rosemary and sage, and roast at 200C for about 30 minutes, turning every 10 minutes so they brown on all sides.

🍽 Serve with the roasts or alone with a spicy tomato and chilli salsa.

Serves 6

BEEF RUMP

I'm astounded at the lack of choice in the meat cabinets of most supermarkets. The subtle art of the butcher just doesn't seem to feature in the shrink-wrapped world of the chiller. The problem for me is the lack of someone to discuss and advise and ultimately prepare a specific cut, and that someone has traditionally been the butcher.

Every community and town still has at least one and the best part of visiting the butcher is discussing what you are going to buy. I like beef rump for its flavour and lately the rump cap has been a preference. As its name suggests, it sits on top of the rump. Marbling runs along it ensuring great flavour and it's very tender if cooked properly.

If I phone ahead, my butcher will keep me a couple of caps. Try doing that at the supermarket!

Beef rump goes with
Extra virgin olive oil; butter; soy sauce; mushroom sauce; red wine sauce; horseradish; wasabi: chilli; balsamic vinegar; parsley; thyme; rosemary; capsicum; roast or grilled vegetables such as parsnip, swede, turnip, potato and carrot; roast garlic; grilled onion; fried leeks; caper; olive; bone marrow.

Slow-roasted beef rump

INGREDIENTS

1 beef rump weighing 3-4kg, trimmed of outer fat
salt and freshly ground black pepper
2 tbsp extra virgin olive oil

METHOD

- This is a method of cooking meat championed by British chef Heston Blumenthal. As long as the core temperature of the meat doesn't exceed 55C, it will stay moist and juicy.
- Preheat the oven to 55C. Use an oven thermometer to make sure the temperature doesn't exceed this. Rub the olive oil onto the surface of the rump and season the beef with salt and pepper. Using a blowtorch, brown the meat all over. Browning the meat is important because it won't caramelise in the oven due to the low temperature. If a blowtorch is not available, sear the meat gently in a pan with some oil. Place in a roasting tray and roast for 20 hours. This will take a little foresight in planning when you sit down to eat, but the rump will hold well for an hour or two as long as the temperature is reduced to 50C or a little lower.

Serves 8-12

Grilled beef rump cap with roast garlic, horseradish and sage

INGREDIENTS

2 beef rump caps, each
  weighing around 300-400g,
  trimmed by your butcher
2 whole bulbs of garlic
4-5cm piece of fresh
  horseradish
2 tbsp extra virgin olive oil (for
  horseradish)
handful of sage leaves
3 tbsp extra virgin olive oil (for
  the rump cap)
salt and freshly ground pepper

METHOD

 Remove the rump caps from the refrigerator and bring them to room temperature. Preheat the oven to 160C. Place the garlic bulbs on an oven tray and roast until the cloves feel soft – about 20 minutes. Remove from the oven and cool a little before peeling the cloves carefully so they stay whole. Roasting the garlic keeps its flavour but won't repeat once eaten. Turn the oven down to 50C.

 Lightly peel the horseradish stem and grate it using a fine grater. Mix with the olive oil. Season both sides of the rump caps with a little salt and pepper. Heat 2 tablespoons of the remaining olive oil in a large frypan, on a moderate flame, and fry the rump caps for 2 minutes on each side. Remove the caps from the pan and place them on an oven tray in the warm oven to rest. Meanwhile, turn up the heat in the pan and add half a cup of water and the sage leaves. Bring to the boil and reduce to a few tablespoons. Strain through a fine sieve into a small saucepan and bring to a simmer. Add the last tablespoon of extra virgin olive oil and turn down to a low heat. Slice the rump caps and serve with the accompaniments.

Serves 4

Leftover roast rump winter salad

INGREDIENTS

400g leftover roast rump, sliced thinly
handful parsley leaves
6 basil leaves
1 tbsp capers, washed well
2 pickled gherkins
4 pickled onions
1 slice bread, crusts removed
4 tbsp red wine vinegar
1 hard boiled egg, peeled, white and yolk separated
4 tbsp extra virgin olive oil
salt and pepper
4 lemon wedges

METHOD

 Finely chop the parsley, basil, capers, gherkins and onions. Put them in a bowl. In a small dish soak the bread in the vinegar for 10 minutes then mash it with a fork, along with the egg yolk, before adding to the chopped ingredients. Mix well, slowly adding the olive oil to obtain a fairly fluid mixture. Season with salt and pepper before adding the finely chopped egg white. Mix gently and spoon the sauce over the plated slices of beef rump.

 Serve with the lemon wedges.

Serves 4

COOKING IN CLAY

Afghan bakers carry on a tradition of cooking in clay ovens that goes back to Neolithic times, when people dug hearth ovens in the ground and packed smooth, wet clay on the sides to stabilise them. The theory goes that as they cooked the food, using stones heated on hot coals at the bottom of these pit ovens, the clay was fired hard and pottery was born.

Food cooks differently in clay. When vegetables are roasted in the oven in a metal baking dish, most of the heat is concentrated on the metal surface, quickly burning anything in contact with it. You've got to be careful you don't dry those vegetables out and char them. Roast them in a clay baking dish and they remain moist, cooking more evenly because of the way the heat is distributed.

Care must be taken when using terracotta pots and dishes to avoid what's called thermal shock. I've lost one Moroccan tagine due to inexperience but now that I know its limits this clay pot is one of my most used.

Before use the clay pot must be seasoned. Do this by immersing it in water overnight. Remove it the next day and place in a cold oven. Turn the heat up to 150C for 90 minutes until it's dry. Remove it from the oven and place it on a wooden surface or a dry cloth to cool. Don't put it onto a cold surface such as marble or stainless steel.

Clay pots work best in the even heat of an oven but I've found that I can lightly fry on my tagine base if I use a medium flame on a heat diffuser and then finish the dish in the oven. That's after the tagine has been constantly used in the oven for a few months.

Sweet potato roasted with sesame seed and thyme

INGREDIENTS

700g red sweet potato

100ml extra virgin olive oil

½ cup sesame seeds

¼ cup fresh thyme, taken off the stem

salt and pepper

METHOD

🍽 Peel the sweet potato and cut into 4cm-thick rounds then cut each into semicircles. Place into a large bowl with all the other ingredients and mix well. Tip the contents into a clay baking dish and arrange the sweet potato pieces evenly along the bottom. Use a spatula to get all the oil, sesame and thyme out of the bowl and onto the sweet potato. Place into a preheated 200C oven for 50-70 minutes till tender.

Serves 6-8

Beef shoulder cooked in clay

INGREDIENTS

2kg piece of beef shoulder, trimmed of any tough skin

100ml extra virgin olive oil

3 garlic cloves, peeled and cut into chunks

4 onions, peeled and chopped into chunks

4 carrots, peeled and chopped into chunks

2 sticks celery, chopped into chunks

1.5 litres red wine

sprig rosemary about 4cm long

2 bay leaves

5 cloves

3-4 good pinches salt

1 tsp freshly cracked pepper

METHOD

🍽 Tie the piece of beef shoulder (your butcher will do this) so it remains neat as it cooks. Heat the olive oil in a pan and brown the meat so it is well coloured. Transfer the meat to a clay pot with a lid. Add the vegetables to the pan and lightly fry for 3-4 minutes. Add half a cup of the red wine so that it bubbles and deglazes the pan. Pour the small amount of liquid and the vegetables into the clay pot containing the meat. Add the rosemary, bay leaves and cloves as well as 3-4 good pinches of salt and a teaspoon of freshly cracked pepper. Add the rest of the red wine and seal with the lid.

🍽 Place in a preheated 160C oven for 3 hours. Once cooked, remove the meat and slice it. Strain the sauce and reduce it by boiling if still a little thin.

🍽 Serve the meat with the sauce on top.

Serves 10

Slow-cooked rabbit with red wine

INGREDIENTS

8 tbsp extra virgin olive oil

1 white onion, peeled and diced

6 garlic cloves, roughly chopped

100g piece of prosciutto, cut into 1cm cubes

200g firm green olives, pitted and halved

1 rabbit weighing 1.2-1.5kg, jointed

3-4 good pinches salt

500ml red wine

3 tbsp good quality balsamic vinegar

1 cup roughly chopped Italian parsley

freshly cracked pepper

METHOD

🍽 Place a well-seasoned clay braising pot on a medium flame and heat the olive oil. Add the onions, garlic, prosciutto and olives. Fry until the onions are transparent. Add the rabbit pieces. Add 3-4 good pinches of salt and mix everything together well. Add enough wine so that the rabbit is almost covered. Place a lid on the pot and transfer to a preheated 150C oven for 4 hours. After this time add the balsamic vinegar and the parsley, seasoning with a little more salt (if needed) and some freshly cracked pepper. Rest for 5 minutes before plating.

Serves 4-6

Cooking in clay is good for
Red and white wine; rabbit; long slow braises; shoulder cuts of lamb, pork and beef; chicken; guineafowl; chickpeas; all manner of dried beans such as cannellini, borlotti and broad beans; lentils; balsamic vinegar; parmesan crusts.

DRIED BEANS

Some years ago, while driving along the Pacific Highway, we turned off just south of Woodburn in northern NSW at a curious sign pointing to "New Italy". It led to a museum of sorts documenting the founding of a settlement there by 20 Italian families that had arrived by boat in Sydney in 1881. Sir Henry Parkes allowed them to stay and even granted part of the substantial acreage now known as New Italy. Attached to the museum we found a cafe with a small but traditional menu. This may not seem out of the ordinary but if you've ever travelled Highway 1, you'll know what a wasteland it is for decent food. One dish in particular we had that day, a bean dish called pasta e fagioli (pasta and beans), always reminds me of New Italy.

Pasta e fagioli is perhaps Italy's most famous bean dish and typifies the rich tradition of using various types of dried beans in its culinary heritage. Not even Catherine de Medici's attempts to refine Italian cooking along the lines of the French court could diminish their place as a cornerstone of Italian cuisine.

Dried beans need at least 8 hours soaking, although 12 hours are preferable. Pick out any beans that are discoloured and cover under 3-4cm of cold water. Any that float are probably too old and should be discarded. Always drain and rinse the beans before using and never use the soaking water for cooking. Simmer beans gently so they retain their shape.

Dried beans go with
Most herbs and spices as well as aromatic vegetables such as onion, garlic, celery, carrot; sausages and rich meats such as pork, duck, veal and lamb shanks are particularly suited; robust-flavoured fish and crustaceans such as barramundi, trout and salmon, scallops and crayfish.

Dried fava bean puree

INGREDIENTS

400g dried, skinned and split fava, or broad beans
8 garlic cloves, peeled and left whole
1 medium-sized red onion, coarsely chopped
½ cup fennel tops, chopped or 1 tsp fennel seeds
4 dried tomatoes, mashed in ¼ cup water
¼ cup extra virgin olive oil
salt and pepper

METHOD

🍽 Soak the beans overnight. Drain, rinse and place the beans in a pot, just covered with fresh water. Add the garlic, onion, fennel and dried tomato mixture. Simmer, covered, until everything is soft and falling apart. Mash everything with a fork but still allow little "bits" for texture – don't put in a blender. Season with salt and pepper and mix in the olive oil. Serve as an alternative to mashed potato.

Serves 4-6

Chicken with borlotti beans

INGREDIENTS

1 cup dried borlotti beans, soaked overnight
4 tbsp extra virgin olive oil
4 chicken legs, thigh and drumstick separated
salt and pepper
4 garlic cloves, chopped
sprig each rosemary and sage
150ml red wine
250ml chicken stock
150ml tomato passato (puree)
½ cup flat-leaf parsley, roughly chopped

METHOD

🍽 Drain the soaking beans and wash them well. Place them in a pot and cover with water. Bring to the boil, turn down and simmer, covered, for an hour or so until the beans are tender. Drain and set aside.

🍽 Heat the olive oil in a wide frypan and fry the chicken pieces, seasoned with salt and pepper, on both sides for 3-4 minutes till well browned. Add the garlic, rosemary and sage and keep frying for a minute or so, moving the chicken around. Add the wine and turn the heat up high.

🍽 When the liquid has almost all evaporated, add the broth and the passato. Turn down to a simmer, cover with a lid and cook slowly for 15 minutes. Remove the lid and add the cooked borlotti beans and the parsley. Simmer for 10 minutes more. Check for seasoning and serve.

Serves 4

Baked beans with meatballs

INGREDIENTS

Meatballs

150g minced pork shoulder

150g minced veal shoulder

2 garlic cloves, finely chopped

1 egg

50g finely grated parmesan

½ cup flat-leaf parsley, finely
chopped

2-3 good pinches salt

½ tsp fine white pepper

Beans

3 tbsp extra virgin olive oil

100g prosciutto or pancetta,
finely diced

1 onion, finely chopped

2 garlic cloves, minced

200ml red wine

800g dried beans, such as
lima, butter or borlotti,
soaked overnight

15 sage leaves, whole

2 bay leaves

500g pureed canned tomatoes

salt and freshly cracked pepper

METHOD

For the meatballs, combine all the meatball ingredients. Roll into balls about 2.5cm in diameter and refrigerate until needed.

For the beans, heat the olive oil in an ovenproof dish and lightly fry the prosciutto, onions and garlic for 2-3 minutes. Add the red wine and cook until the liquid reduces by half. Add the drained beans, herbs and tomatoes and season with 2-3 good pinches of salt. Mix well. Cover with a lid and bake in a preheated 140C oven for 60-90 minutes until beans are cooked. Add the meatballs to the dish, distributing evenly and carefully covering with some of the liquid. Add some cracked pepper and return to the oven for 15-20 minutes. Serve hot with bread.

Serves 6-8

GUAVA

There are guava trees all over Sydney, in backyards and streets. We had a cherry guava in our garden when I was growing up.

There are many species of guava, all sharing a distinctive sweet perfume that is instantly recognisable as tropical. But each has a slightly different nuance that, I suspect, has given rise to their individual names. Perhaps the sweetest are the smaller fruits, those of the yellow and red cherry guavas, no larger than 3cm. The larger Indian white has flavours of banana, while the pink (Hawaiian) is more tutti-frutti.

Botanically, it's related to the fragrant myrtle, with close ties to some of the most aromatic plants such as allspice, eucalyptus and clove. When under-ripe, guava has a wild, musky, almost animal-like quality but when allowed to develop that offputting feral smell is replaced by a rich, sweet scent.

Guava flesh is thick and pleasantly gritty – the Aztecs called it xalxcotl (sand plum). That texture is immediately apparent in one of the many bottled juices made from either white or pink varieties as well as guava paste.

The fruit has a seedy centre that, in some varieties, can be annoying. Peeling, pureeing and sieving solves this problem and produces a thick, creamy puree that can be frozen. The puree is perfect for folding into cream, custard and yoghurt or swirling through icecream or gelato. I like to layer sponge or teacake with sweetened puree.

The fresh fruit can be eaten as is or simmered with vanilla, sugar and water or sweet wine, then cooled and served with rice or tapioca pudding. Guava paste can be used wherever quince paste is used, especially with soft white cheeses or a robust blue.

White guava cream

INGREDIENTS

240g peeled white guava (about 265g whole)
3 tbsp caster sugar
120ml cream

METHOD

🍽 Puree the guava in a food processor with the sugar. Pass through a fine sieve. Whip the cream to stiff peaks and fold in the guava puree. Can be used as a filling for sponge cake, served in a bowl with sponge fingers or spread onto toasted fruit bread.

Serves 4

Pink guava jam

INGREDIENTS

2kg pink guava
1.3kg sugar
juice of 1 lemon

METHOD

🍽 Peel the guavas and remove the seeds. Put peels and seeds into a pot, cover them with water and bring to the boil, then simmer for 10 minutes. Cut the guava flesh into small pieces and put them in another pot with the sugar and lemon juice. Strain the water from the peels and seeds and add it to the guava flesh and sugar. Bring to the boil then turn down to a bubbling simmer.

🍽 Cook till the jam thickens. Check this by putting a small teaspoon of the jam on a cold plate. Tip it at an angle. If it is ready it will set.

Makes 2 litres jam

Guava goes with

Lime and lemon juice; rum; coconut; dark sugars such as muscovar and demerara; mint; almonds; walnuts; macadamia; cream; stone fruit such as apricot, peach, nectarine and cherry.

Guava and macadamia torte

INGREDIENTS

100g caster sugar, plus 2 tbsp extra

120g macadamia nuts

400g peeled ripe pink guava (about 450g whole)

4 tbsp OP rum

125g unsalted butter

1 egg

150g plain flour

1 tsp baking powder

pinch salt

¼ cup apricot jam

METHOD

🍴 Finely grind 2 tablespoons of sugar and the macadamias in a food processor, remove and set aside. Set aside two guavas and place the rest in the food processor. Halve the reserved guava lengthways and scoop out the seedy pulp with a small spoon. Add this pulp to the processor. Meanwhile, cut the four halves into four slices each and set aside. Add 2 tablespoons of rum to the guava pulp and puree in the processor then pass through a sieve.

🍴 Butter and flour a 24cm cake pan and preheat the oven to 190C. In a mixer, cream the butter and the sugar.

🍴 Add the egg and mix till fluffy. Add the guava puree. Sift flour, baking powder and salt together and add a little at a time on low speed. Finally, add the sugar and nuts. Spread the mixture evenly in the pan and press the guava slices randomly on top.

🍴 Bake for 30 minutes. In a saucepan bring the apricot jam and remaining rum to a simmer till liquid. After it's cooked, glaze the torte with a brush while hot. Cool before serving.

Makes 24cm torte

LEMONS

Lemons are available to us year-round but from late autumn to spring they are at their best. In winter, I rely on their antiseptic quality by mixing the juice of a lemon with a spoonful of honey and hot water to soothe my throat.

We've learnt to use lemon's acidity in the kitchen, from its ability to prevent discolouration in peeled artichokes, bananas and pears to adjusting flavour balance in dressings, sauces and emulsions such as mayonnaise. We can also use that acidity to cook without heat.

Thinly sliced raw fish, marinated in lemon juice and olive oil with other flavourings, such as garlic, capers, onion and olive, if left for 30 minutes or more will "cook". The flesh turns opaque and milky. The same principle can be applied to most seafood but it must be fresh.

A favourite lemon of cooks and gardeners alike is the meyer. You'll spot it (though rarely in the shops because it is thin-skinned and difficult to transport) by its roundness and its sweet, floral perfume. Its juice is markedly less acidic than that of other lemons but for flavouring in tarts, biscuits and cakes the meyer is unrivalled.

Much of the fragrance of a lemon is in the skin, which contains the essential oils. The popular Italian liqueur limoncello is made using peel from lemons that are turning from green to yellow. To capture that fragrance, simply grate lemon zest into dressings, tagines and braises or even onto ossobuco.

Lemons go with
Veal, lamb; chicken; duck; fish and shellfish; fish sauce; sugar; cream; eggs; oranges; mango; stone fruits; papaya; guava; strawberries; spinach; mushrooms; chillies; noodles; rice; coriander; parsley; beans; artichokes; avocado; pancakes; grappa and rum.

Salsa salmoriglio

INGREDIENTS

juice of 2 lemons
zest of 1 lemon
1 cup extra virgin olive oil
1 garlic clove, minced
1 cup flat-leaf parsley, chopped
2 tbsp fresh oregano leaves, roughly chopped
salt and pepper

METHOD

- This classic Sicilian lemon, garlic and olive salsa is used to dress grilled seafood and barbecued meats. It is also very good as an alternative dressing for cooked vegetables or a fennel and orange salad. The quality of the salsa depends to a great degree on the quality of the olive oil used and being made fresh each day as the lemon juice oxidises quickly.
- Whisk the lemon juice and olive oil together. Add all the other ingredients and mix well. Season to taste with salt and pepper and allow to sit for at least an hour.

Makes 2 cups salsa

Trout fillets in lemon butter

INGREDIENTS

200g green beans, topped and tailed
2 tbsp extra virgin olive oil
1 garlic clove, minced
¼ cup parsley, finely chopped
rind of 1 lemon, finely grated
100g unsalted butter
4 river trout fillets, skin left on
juice of 2 lemons
salt and pepper

METHOD

- Bring a pot of salted water to the boil and blanch the beans for 5 minutes till soft. Drain and dress with the olive oil, garlic, parsley and lemon rind while still hot. Season and toss. Heat half the butter in a frypan until it starts to foam. Season the trout fillets with salt and pepper and fry carefully in the butter for a minute or two per side. Remove the pan from the heat and keep the fillets warm. In a smaller frypan add the rest of the butter with a pinch of salt. Fry until it is nut brown then add the lemon juice. Serve the fillets with the butter and lemon sauce accompanied by the beans.

Serves 4

Lemon semolina biscuits

INGREDIENTS

110g unsalted butter

200g plain flour

100g semolina

1 tsp baking powder

½ tsp bicarb soda (baking soda)

pinch salt

2 tbsp extra virgin olive oil

200g sugar

1 egg

1 egg yolk

grated zest and juice of 1 lemon

½ tsp vanilla extract

60g sugar, for rolling

METHOD

🍽 Soften the butter by leaving it at room temperature for 30 minutes. Mix together, in a bowl, the flour, semolina, baking powder, bicarb soda and salt, and set aside. Cream together the butter, olive oil and 200g of sugar in an electric mixer, using the paddle attachment, until light and fluffy. Add the egg, yolk, vanilla, lemon zest and juice until well combined (may be necessary to scrape down the sides).

🍽 On low speed add the dry ingredients set aside and mix till soft dough is formed. Wrap the dough in some cling film, flatten into a disc and refrigerate for 90 minutes. Preheat the oven to 170C. Put the 60g of sugar in a bowl.

🍽 Using lightly floured fingers, take a small piece of dough and roll each biscuit to the size of a golf ball. Roll each ball in the sugar and place on baking sheets covered with baking paper. Each ball should be about 4cm from the other. Bake for 20-25 minutes till lightly golden.

🍽 Cool and store in airtight containers.

Makes about 40 biscuits

PRAWNS

The banana prawn is caught year round, with peak supply in April and the bulk coming from the Northern Prawn Fishery stretching from the Gulf of Carpentaria all the way west to the Kimberley.

King prawns, especially the eastern king, are in season throughout summer while tiger prawns are caught between August and November. Of the three, banana prawns have the softest texture and, if in good condition, they can be the sweetest of all. Of course, if any prawn is overcooked it will dry out and develop a rubbery texture.

Pre-cooked prawns can be convenient, especially if filling a crusty roll or tossing in a salad, but care should be taken when cooking or even heating them again. When adding pre-cooked prawns to a pasta sauce or a curry, toss them in at the very end. The idea is to heat them gently.

Care should also be taken with green (raw) prawns. Their texture and flavour are best when they are just cooked. If adding to a curry, a soup or a stew, then simmer for 5 minutes at most. When barbecuing prawns in their shell give them, at most, a minute or two a side, depending on size. Shelled prawns should take 30 seconds to a minute each side, again, depending on size.

Prawns go with

Garlic; chives; spring onion; ginger; chilli; mirin (rice wine); fish sauce; soy sauce; coriander; cumin; basil; oregano; lime and lemon; Sichuan pepper; tomato; iceberg lettuce; cucumber; mayonnaise, especially garlic; red and yellow capsicum; eggs, scrambled eggs and omelettes.

Prawn stock

INGREDIENTS

heads and shells from 1.2kg prawns
1 small leek, cut into 5mm thick rounds
1 small carrot, peeled and cut into 2cm rounds
2 sticks celery
1 cup tomato puree
3 garlic cloves, peeled and left whole

METHOD

- Bring a pot of water to the boil and blanch the prawn shells and heads for 20-30 seconds.
- Drain and put the prawn shells into a stockpot with the leek, carrot, celery, tomato and garlic. Cover with cold water and bring to the boil. Turn down the heat and simmer for 1 hour, skimming any scum from the surface.
- Strain and it is ready to use.

Makes about 2 litres of stock

Prawns with potatoes and tarragon

INGREDIENTS

8 tbsp extra virgin olive oil
1 stem of tarragon
handful parsley, roughly chopped
800g green king prawns, peeled and deveined
400g waxy yellow potatoes, skin on and boiled
2 garlic cloves, peeled and sliced
4 tbsp chives, finely chopped
6 sage leaves
3 tbsp red wine vinegar
salt and pepper

METHOD

- In a pot, preferably clay, heat 6 tablespoons of the olive oil, the tarragon and half the parsley on a low flame. After a couple of minutes, add the peeled prawns with a couple of good pinches of salt and a turn or two of pepper. Let them cook for 6-8 minutes.
- Peel the potatoes and put them in a bowl, still warm, with the rest of the oil, parsley, chives, sage and vinegar. Add a little salt and crush with the back of a fork. Distribute the potato among four plates and make a wide well in each.
- Spoon the prawns evenly on top of each crater of potato and dress with the cooking oil.

Serves 4

Prawn and barley stew

INGREDIENTS

250g pearled barley

4 tbsp extra virgin olive oil

4 shallots, peeled and thinly sliced

3 garlic cloves, peeled and crushed

½ tsp smoked paprika

¼ tsp chilli powder

1 tsp fennel seed

1 cup dry white wine

1 litre prawn stock (see prawn stock recipe)

2 cups tomato passato (puree)

3 banana chillies, seeded and halved

2 litres water

300g shelled peas

1.2kg medium king prawns, shelled and deveined

1 cup chopped parsley

salt and pepper

METHOD

Place barley in a sieve and wash quickly under running water to remove dust or dirt. Heat olive oil in a large pot and gently fry shallots, garlic, paprika, chilli powder and fennel for a minute. Add wine, turn up heat and boil until there is almost no liquid left. Add prawn stock and passato, banana chillies and a litre of water. Bring to boil and add barley. Simmer for 15 minutes then add peas. Simmer for 15 minutes more then add prawns. Cook for 5 minutes then add parsley. Season with salt and pepper to taste and stir well. Serve hot.

Serves 8

Note: Leftover stew can be excellent a day or two after being made though the barley will have absorbed the liquid. Reheat by adding a cup of water and a quarter cup of tomato puree and gently bringing to the boil. More prawns or other seafood can be added to make a "leftovers" meal.

FLOUNDER

W hy are fish so thin? Because they eat other fish. Boom-tish.

Jerry Seinfeld may well have been thinking about the flounder when he delivered that joke, because as fish go they are among the thinnest. Their flat shape and ability to camouflage themselves by changing colour make them perfectly suited to lurking on sandy sea floors and muddy inshore areas.

The flounder's thinness is also an advantage when it comes to cooking. Unlike chunkier fish, its flat shape means it cooks quickly and relatively evenly. The fillets are pearly white when cooked and have a delicately sweet flavour.

But for me, there's something especially satisfying about eating fish on the bone. It tastes better because the bones keep it moist and prevent the flesh from shrinking.

To cook flounder whole, it has to be gutted and skinned. The first is easy to do – just ask your fishmonger to do it for you.

Skinning is only marginally more difficult than gutting. Lay the flounder on a board. With a sharp knife, make an incision across the point just before the flesh ends and the tail starts. Using the knife, prise a little of the skin away from the flesh at the incision point, just enough so you can get a grip with your fingers. Put a little salt on your fingertips and, holding the tail with one hand, peel away the skin with the other towards the head. Repeat the process on the other side.

Flounder fillets in tomato and capsicum

INGREDIENTS

600g flounder fillets
3 tbsp extra virgin olive oil
1 medium onion, finely sliced
2 garlic cloves, minced
2 red capsicums, cored and
    finely sliced
1 tsp fresh thyme
200g peeled ripe tomatoes,
    chopped
salt and pepper

METHOD

- In a large pan, lightly fry flounder fillets in oil for 30 seconds a side and set them aside on a plate. In same pan, fry onion, garlic and capsicum for 2 minutes until soft. Add thyme and tomatoes and simmer gently for 5 minutes. Season with salt and pepper, mix well and add cooked flounder fillets.
- Spoon sauce over fillets so they are covered as much as possible and simmer for another minute before serving.

Serves 4

Flounder gratin

INGREDIENTS

4 flounder, each around 250g,
    peeled
4 tbsp extra virgin olive oil
½ cup parsley, finely chopped
1 garlic clove, minced
4 tbsp breadcrumbs
4 tbsp grated parmesan
salt

METHOD

- Coat the fish well with the olive oil and place them in an ovenproof tray. Mix the parsley, garlic, breadcrumbs and parmesan together and distribute evenly on each fish. Season with salt and place in a preheated 180C oven for 15-20 minutes.
- Remove and serve immediately with slices of lemon.

Serves 4

Flounder goes with
Butter; extra virgin olive oil; batter; breadcrumbs; herbs such as coriander, parsley, thyme and tarragon; fennel seeds; olives; capers; chilli; ginger; garlic; wasabi; light soy sauce; salad leaves especially the bitter ones like radicchio, rocket and endive; tomato; cucumber; zucchini; celery heart; potatoes; spinach; cabbage; pickled vegetables.

Flounder with olives and lemon

INGREDIENTS

2 whole flounder, gutted and
  skinned, heads removed

50g plain flour

4 tbsp extra virgin olive oil

1 garlic clove, minced

20 good quality small black
  olives, pitted

1 small lemon, well washed
  and cut into 6-8 slices

handful of flat-leaf parsley,
  chopped

salt and freshly cracked pepper

METHOD

- Dredge flounder in flour so both sides are well dusted. Tap off excess. Heat 3 tablespoons of the olive oil in a large frypan, on a medium heat, and add flounder. (Do them one at a time if your pan is not large enough. If so, set your oven to 100C to keep the cooked flounder warm as you fry the other.) The fish should take 90 seconds to 2 minutes a side to cook.

- Once done, place fish on warm plates. Tip oil out of the pan and heat remaining tablespoon in the same pan. Add garlic and fry gently until soft. Add half a cup of water as well as olives, lemon slices and parsley. Turn up heat and evaporate liquid until just a few tablespoons are left.

- Season sauce with salt and freshly cracked pepper, then spoon over flounder.

Serves 2

INDEX